Global Activism in
an American School

Global Activism in an American School

From Empathy to Action

Linda Kantor Swerdlow

To Pat,
Enjoy the
book!
Linda K Swerdlow

ROWMAN & LITTLEFIELD
Lanham • Boulder • New York • London

Published by Rowman & Littlefield
A wholly owned subsidiary of The Rowman & Littlefield Publishing Group, Inc.
4501 Forbes Boulevard, Suite 200, Lanham, Maryland 20706
www.rowman.com

Unit A, Whitacre Mews, 26-34 Stannary Street, London SE11 4AB

British Library Cataloguing in Publication Information Available

Library of Congress Cataloging-in-Publication Data

Names: Swerdlow, Linda Kantor, author.
Title: Global activism in an American school : from empathy to action /
    Linda Kantor Swerdlow.
Description: Lanham, Maryland : Rowman & Littlefield, 2016. |
    Includes bibliographical references.
Identifiers: LCCN 2016027100 (print) | LCCN 2016040271 (ebook) |
    ISBN 9781475807691 (cloth : alk. paper) | ISBN 9781475807707
    (pbk. : alk. paper) | ISBN 9781475807714 (electronic)
Subjects: LCSH: Students—United States—Political activity. | Broad Meadows
    Middle School (Quincy, Mass.)—Political activity. | Humanitarian assistance—
    United States—Case studies. | School buildings—Developing countries—
    Design and construction. | Child workers—Abuse of—Developing countries.
Classification: LCC LB3610 .S96 2016 (print) | LCC LB3610 (ebook) | DDC
    371.8/10973—dc23
LC record available at https://lccn.loc.gov/2016027100

Printed in the United States of America

*This book is dedicated to my parents,
John and Marion Kantor*

Contents

Foreword

Ron Adams and the middle school students who worked on The Kid's Campaign to Build a School for Iqbal and Operation Day's Work, Linda Kantor Swerdlow, and I all strongly believe that global child labor needs to be combated and eradicated. It is through this shared belief and our desire to raise awareness of the issue that our paths crossed.

I am an occupational physician and epidemiologist in Minneapolis, Minnesota. Over the last 25 years, I have photographed children working in a variety of occupations around the world. In general, work conditions in developing nations are far inferior to those in developed nations. Health problems are compounded for children who are more susceptible to occupational hazards than are adults. For example, children have many more years to develop dust-related lung diseases than do adults from arduous work in brick factories and stone quarries. Children contract unknown illnesses from working inside chemical-filled leather tanning drums and carpet weavers may suffer from the development of degenerative joint disease by the age of 12.

Like other adults who work to raise awareness of global child labor, I was shocked and saddened by the murder of 12-year-old Iqbal Masih, the Pakistani former child laborer-turned activist. I learned about the campaign of 7th-grade teacher Ron Adams and the students at Broad Meadows Middle School in Quincy, Massachusetts, to build a school in memory of Iqbal, who had visited the school three months earlier and decided to lend my support.

Sometime in the later part of 1997 or early 1998, I had been invited by Rita Braver and CBS Sunday to participate in a short documentary about my photographic work on child labor. During my initial phone interview with Ms. Braver, I suggested that we link the production to a talk at the

Broad Meadows school and an exhibition at the Lowell National Historical Park—a combined exhibition of my work and that of Lewis Hine, a social documentary photographer who exposed child labor in the United States in the early part of the 20th century.

The idea that access to a good education is a necessity and a right of every child has sprung from the growing concern that not all children are provided equal educational opportunities and do not grow up free from economic exploitation. In spite of the many international treaties, child labor remains a problem of enormous magnitude and basic education remains out of reach for many millions of children. Today over 85 million children work in the worst forms of child labor, many as slave or bonded laborers.

Unlike many important human rights and environmental problems, children and young adults readily understand the inherent inequity in child labor. However, Iqbal didn't just visit Broad Meadows by chance in 1994. As *Global Activism in an American School: From Empathy to Action* documents, Ron Adams' innovative teaching and community-building strategies set the stage for the democratic student-centered programs that would continue for over 25 years.

I wonder what would have happened if Iqbal had not visited Broad Meadows or if another teacher had been there when Iqbal arrived. Did Ron always believe he could teach children that they could lasso the moon? Readers of this book can ask themselves if it was Ron or Iqbal that inspired a generation of activists. I have thought about asking his perspective on that question, but it is rare to have an Iqbal visit, and certainly neither Iqbal Masih nor Malala Yousafzai can visit every school. Perhaps his day with the Broad Meadows students provided a community for Iqbal as much as it was a place for him to visit.

Today, over 20 years after his death, Iqbal's voice is still heard at the Broad Meadows Middle School. Due to the success of The Kid's Campaign to Build a School for Iqbal, Broad Meadows was selected as a pilot school by the United States Agency for International Development (USAID) for the American adaption of Operation Day's Work (ODW), the highly successful Norwegian youth activist program. Through ODW, Ron Adams has brought together middle school students to help them find their voices and engage in global human rights activism. Over the years, Mr. Adams and his students have met with global leaders, visited Congress, built a school in Pakistan, and generally followed their vision for a just world.

Perhaps The Kid's Campaign to Build a School for Iqbal and Operation Day's Work can best be seen as building justice one child at a time.

However, they are really more than that; it is how the students work together to create something—or things—that is much greater than the individual parts—a synergistic learning experience.

—David Parker, Senior Medical Researcher, Health Partners Institute
Author of *Before Their Time: The World of Child Labor*;
By these Hands: Portraits from the Factory Floor;
and *Stolen Dreams: Portraits of Working Children*

Acknowledgments

There are so many people I want to thank for their help and support. I must start with the folks from Quincy, Massachusetts. First and foremost, Ron Adams, for answering my endless questions, allowing me to observe at ODW meetings and events, and introducing me to his former students and their parents. I also want to thank his former students and the parents who shared their experiences: Amanda, Jen, Ellaine, the entire Bloomer family, Mike, Rita, Mia, Connor, Brandi, and Amy as well as Dr. Ed Fitzgerald, the Director of the Quincy Historical Society; and Mary Clark and Anne McLaughlin of the Thomas Crane Library in Quincy.

My colleagues at Drew University were also key. My Deans: Robert Ready, Bill Rogers, and Edye Lawler for their ongoing support; the MAT staff, Gail Hilliard Nelson, Amy Saks Pavese, and Dawn LoMauro for creating the collegial environment that makes writing possible; and the graduate students who transcribed the interview tapes: Jackie Harte, Marja Anderson, Doug Oswin, Siobhan Kinealy, and Caeli Beckhert.

I also want to thank Chris Campisano, Margaret Michelli, and Frank Sedita for reading and commenting on segments of the book and Sarah Jubar, my editor at Rowman and Littlefield, for her patience and encouragement throughout.

My dear friends Margaret Michelli and Meera Rao helped me through with all the support and encouragement that they always provide. Last but not least, my heartfelt thanks goes to my wonderful family: my son Ben Swerdlow and my husband Mike Swerdlow. Without them, this book would not have come to fruition. They gave me their full support, read drafts, and discussed problems I encountered along the way. They pushed me to keep going when I felt stuck and provided the care and support that helped me to flourish. I can't thank them enough.

Introduction

On Friday afternoon, after the school bell rings, it is common to see 20–30 middle school students crowd into Ron Adams' classroom at Broad Meadows Middle School in Quincy, Massachusetts. The first order of the day is snacks and Mr. Adams, a 7th grade English teacher, proudly tells the students that the beverages and pretzels have been donated by community members who support the good work that the students are doing.

As the students begin to relax, they move into seats in the oblong classroom that once served as a science lab. The atmosphere is informal and they sit any way they choose, at the desks, atop the desks, or along the side counters near the sinks. The room is decorated with student work and memorabilia from youth activist campaigns that have evolved in this room in years past. Once the debris from the snacks has been collected, two 8th graders move to the front of the room and begin the weekly meeting of Operation Day's Work (ODW).

BEGINNINGS

I first met Ron Adams and two of his students, Kristin and Tom, in Washington, DC during the summer of 2005. The middle school students were presenting at a two-day workshop on Global Child Labor. The workshop was geared toward teachers and teacher educators and its purpose was to provide us with resources and teaching ideas to develop educational campaigns in our respective programs. The event was sponsored by the International Center on Child Labor and Education (ICCLE) and funded by the US Department of Labor.

As a teacher educator interested in youth activism, I was intrigued by Kristen and Tom's presentation. The students were passionate about ending child labor and had a strong sense of social justice, unusual for students so young. Over dinner, Ron shared the story of global activism at Broad Meadows Middle School.

When 12-year-old Iqbal Masih, a Pakistani former bonded child laborer turned anti-child labor activist, came to Boston in 1994 to receive Reebok's Youth in Action Award, he asked to meet youth his own age. Reebok award organizers selected Broad Meadows Middle School because of its Human Rights curriculum and reputation for student activism. Iqbal's inspirational visit and untimely murder five months later, on his return to Pakistan, inspired the Broad Meadows students to build a school in his memory. The middle school students started a grassroots activist movement, The Kid's Campaign to Build a School for Iqbal.

Brian Atwood, Director of the United States Agency for International Development (USAID), learned of the campaign's success and invited Broad Meadows to become a pilot school for Operation Day's Work, USA (ODW, USA), an American adaptation of Norway's highly effective youth global social action program that the agency hoped to institute in US schools. ODW has been operating successfully as an after school program at Broad Meadows since 1996.

My meeting with Ron and his students touched a raw nerve. During the late 1960s when I was 15, I began to volunteer with the American Committee to Keep Biafra Alive. After school and on weekends, I would take the bus from my home in Clifton, New Jersey, to New York City, where I would work with like-minded youth and adults to canvas, educate, and raise funds to end the genocide in Nigeria. The experiences I had during the two years working to help Biafra were among the most meaningful of my adolescence. I was exposed to ideas and gained skills that shaped my interests and career choice and played an important role in helping me develop a positive identity.

The serendipitous meeting with Ron and his students was in a sense the beginning of a journey. I decided that I wanted to study youth activism that was global or transnational in nature. I hoped to better understand the conditions, program structures, types of teaching and mentoring that inspired students to work for social change on a global level. Given the current emphasis on developing global awareness and 21st-century skills, I was also interested in the long-term impact of participation on the youth who became actively involved.

Ron's programs seemed ideal for such an investigation. I was impressed by the program's longevity (ODW entered its 20th year in 2016) and decided to do a case study of The Kid's Campaign to Build a School for Iqbal and the Broad Meadows chapter of ODW. I kept in touch with Ron and visited Broad Meadows periodically. As a former teacher and current teacher educator, I have spent much of my adult life in classrooms and informal education programs. My visits to Broad Meadows convinced me that I was witnessing something very special.

In 2007, I received a small research grant from Drew University to study the programs at Broad Meadows. I began by conducting ethnographic research and in-depth interviews over a period of 7 years. The research forms the basis of this book.

The book is geared toward practitioners. Forays into theory are intended to demonstrate its uses in applied settings. It also aims to serve as a primer for classroom teachers who wish to start or are looking for ideas to enhance youth civic programs. It is my hope that theory will serve to inform practice and assist practitioners in establishing successful programs.

CONCEPTUAL FRAMEWORK

The programs at Broad Meadows are examined through the lens of situated learning theory. The theory has its antecedents in the experiential learning theory of John Dewey and Lev Vygotsky's social constructivist perspective. Both Dewey and Vygotsky believe that students learn best through active participation in educational activities.

Situated learning theorists think that context (the time and place; the historical and cultural) is an integral part of the learning that occurs. They believe that individuals create knowledge based upon their experiences through collaboration with others in a learning environment.

There are two major approaches to situated learning. The first is rooted in cognitive psychology and education and focuses upon individual understanding. The second is anthropological in its origins and examines how learning occurs within a community. The former focuses upon creating activities: problems or projects that replicate real-world situations and present students with the kinds of cognitive demands they would encounter in the real world. These types of activities are referred to as practice fields, because they aim to create activities that will prepare students for problems they will encounter later on in life. Problem-based learning and simulations are popular types of practice fields (Barb & Duffy, 2012, pp. 29–38).

The anthropological approach is rooted in the work of anthropologist Jean Lave and artificial intelligence researcher Etienne Wenger (1991). Like psychologically oriented situated learning theorists, Lave and Wenger believe that individuals learn best through participating in authentic activities; however, rather than focusing upon educator-created activities, they investigate the manner in which individuals learn and grow through their participation in the changing activities of the communities and institutions in which they are regularly involved.

The model of situated learning that Lave and Wenger developed, Communities of Practice (CoP), will be used to examine the programs at Broad Meadows Middle School. It provides a framework to analyze learning that takes place outside of the classroom in informal settings, such as after school programs or in school projects that require students to work with individuals and/or institutions outside the school to solve real-world problems.

According to Lave and Wenger (1991), a community of practice is comprised of individuals who develop and share practices, beliefs, and understandings as they pursue a common goal to which they are committed over an extended period of time. Examples of CoP include a preservice teacher cohort, an online community devoted to improving chess strategies, or an alcoholic anonymous group.

CoP theory examines how individuals learn and develop specific skills, knowledge, values, and a sense of self or identity through participating in the practices of these communities. According to Lave and Wenger, a community of practice can develop informally or through formal design. It can be hierarchical and power relations can limit or inhibit full participation by all of its members. Or, by evolution or design a more egalitarian community can emerge that offers entry to newcomers through a variety of participatory experiences, mentoring, and informal or even formal apprenticeships. CoPs that move in the direction of intensive or full participation are empowering, while communities that limit or inhibit full participation tend to be disempowering (p. 36).

While The Kid's Campaign and ODW are informal educational programs that take place after (and at times before) school, student activism at Broad Meadows evolved from experimentation and innovation within the classroom. These after school programs are empowering and encourage full participation. However, since they deal with youth and youth-adult relationships, the literature on youth participation and student voice is also explored in order to examine the specific dynamics and issues that emerge in CoP with youth and adult participants.

Both The Kid's Campaign to Build a School for Iqbal and ODW enhance the students' understanding of the global community. However, the idea for ODW and its overarching structure originated in Norway and was brought to this country by USAID specifically for this purpose. In current educational parlance, such understanding or awareness is referred to as global competence. Ironically, ODW, a program devised in Norway during the 1960s and transported to the United States in the 1990s, fosters 21st-century skills and global competencies that experts in the education community currently advocate as essential for American students to solve complex global social problems and to succeed in the increasingly globalized economy of the 21st century.

Academics and educators have used many different terms to refer to global competence. These include intercultural competence, global citizenship, and intercultural sensitivity (Semann & Yamazaki, 2015). In 2011, the Council of Chief State School Officers and the Asia Society Partnership for Global Learning Task force developed a definition and set of competencies that provide a framework for American schools. The task force defines global competence as "the capacity and disposition to act on issues of global significance" (Mansilla & Jackson, p. ix) and identifies the four areas where students need to become proficient in order to become globally competent. Andrews and Conk (2012) refer to the following proficiencies as the four pillars of global competence: "knowledge and inquiry about the world, recognizing and weighing perspectives, communicating ideas, and taking action" (pp. 56–57).

In the United States, educating for global competence is often linked to the development of 21st-century skills. The term refers to a broad set of sophisticated skills that experts believe must become a focal point of the curriculum. These include critical thinking and problem solving, communication, creativity, and collaboration (Trilling, Fadel, & the Partnership for Global Learning, 2009, p. xxvi).

These skills and competencies are fostered through participation in The Kid's Campaign and ODW. These frameworks will be used to analyze the year-long ODW program and will be further developed in later chapters.

RESEARCH METHODOLOGY

When I first met Ron in 2005, ODW was in full swing. Although The Kid's Campaign to Build a School for Iqbal had officially ended, it was clear that both the Campaign and Iqbal's story were very much alive in the hearts and minds of the members of the ODW Broad Meadows chapter. This period in the school's history was a source of pride and was viewed by the ODW members as integral to the current program. Much in the program's structure, rituals, and routines were attributed to The Kid's Campaign. In addition, the issue of global child labor and the Iqbal story were essential parts of the ODW Broad Meadows informal curriculum.

As a researcher, it was evident that I needed to do a case study of these two intertwined programs in order to understand youth activism at Broad Meadows. In order to investigate The Kid's Campaign, I devised an in-depth open-ended interview protocol (Seidman, 2006) and conducted multiple in-depth interviews with Ron Adams and key student participants. I analyzed numerous primary and secondary sources to triangulate the data. Due to the outrage surrounding Iqbal's untimely death and the subsequent media interest in The Kid's Campaign, I was able to access a plethora of sources, including TV interviews with Iqbal and a school video of Iqbal's meeting with the Broad Meadows students in 1994.

While ODW received less media attention, I was able to study the program's operations firsthand. I conducted ethnographic field work over a period of seven years. I observed and documented ODW meetings, speaking engagements, and other events and conducted in-depth interviews with Ron, student activists, the school principal, and parent chaperones (LeCompte & Schensul, 1999). I also collected and analyzed primary and secondary source documents.

Selecting students for the in-depth interviews was a challenge. Potential interview subjects were identified by Ron Adams. He chose students who had been very active and taken on leadership roles in either The Kid's Campaign or ODW for a period of two or more years. From this group, ten students were selected for in-depth study. At the time of the interviews, all were in their twenties or early thirties and during the initial interview indicated that they believed that their participation in The Kid's Campaign and/or ODW had been transformative and strongly influenced the course of their lives. Although limited by sample size, common threads that emerged from the interviews provide valuable insights into the long-term impact of participation in youth activist programs during early adolescence that can lead to further investigations with larger student samples.

In addition to studying The Kid's Campaign and ODW, I conducted historical research on the life of Iqbal Masih, child labor in Pakistan, and the origins of ODW in Norway. The short, tragic life and death of Iqbal Masih has been the subject of controversy and was difficult to research. Susan Kuklin's *Iqbal Masih and the Crusader's Against Child Slavery*, a book geared toward a youth audience, proved to be an invaluable resource. This book, information gleaned from video footage of Iqbal's presentations, and numerous secondary sources provide the basis for the first chapter of the book.

THE PLAN OF THE BOOK

The book is divided into two sections. The first chronicles the development of The Kid's Campaign to Build a School for Iqbal. It lays the groundwork and shows the evolution of the democratic youth activist community programs at Broad Meadows Middle School and their impact on three key student activists and their teacher/mentor Ron Adams.

The second section focuses upon ODW, its development in Norway, and its transition to the United States. It also examines the program's operations and activities over a typical school year at Broad Meadows Middle School and the impact of the program on participants.

CHAPTER 1: PRELUDE: FROM PAKISTAN TO THE USA

The first chapter introduces Iqbal Masih, the 12-year-old Pakistani former child laborer-turned youth activist. His personal story is contextualized through an examination of child labor in Pakistan and the global community. It's a horrific tale and its telling will help the reader to understand the middle school students' shock and desire to take action after being confronted with this "inconvenient truth."

CHAPTER 2: QUINCY, MASSACHUSETTS, USA

Chapter 2 situates The Kid's Campaign and ODW in a broader sociohistorical context. It provides a brief history of the city of Quincy and the school district's early experiments with student-centered learning. It then focuses upon the school community at Broad Meadows Middle School and explores how the structural changes within the school—the shift from a junior high school to a middle school structure and philosophy—empowered the teachers to create course work and curriculum that supports civic efficacy and youth activism.

The chapter's focal point is Ron Adam's development as an educator. It examines the life experiences It examines the life experiences he brings to his teaching and shows how his practice changes and grows more democratic and student centered through participation in informal professional communities and collaborations and in the communities he cocreates with his students.

CHAPTER 3: THE KID'S CAMPAIGN TO BUILD A SCHOOL FOR IQBAL

The student-initiated youth campaign to build a school in the memory of Iqbal Masih is the fruition of Ron Adams' experimentation with youth activism and democratic practice. The chapter explores the evolution of the campaign and its emerging structure that begins to resemble a community of practice. It examines the shifting roles and relations between mentor and students that become the basis of this "youth-centered apprenticeship," as well as the types of learning that take place through participation in this informal community.

CHAPTER 4: IMPACT OF THE KID'S CAMPAIGN
ON THE LIVES OF THE STUDENT ACTIVISTS

This chapter focuses on three student leaders: Amanda, Jen, and Ellaine. It examines the way in which the students' participation in The Kid's Campaign altered the identities, sense of agency, and life choices of these young women who are now in their early thirties.

CHAPTER 5: FROM NORWAY TO THE USA

The chapter examines the development and operation of ODW in Norway. It investigates the program's transition to the United States through the eyes of the members of the Broad Meadows pilot program .A focal point of the chapter is the national ODW USA Constitutional Convention in Philadelphia, and the governing structure developed by the student delegates.

CHAPTER 6: A YEAR IN THE LIFE: PART 1: INVESTIGATING
THE WORLD AND PREPARING TO TAKE ACTION

From September until Thanksgiving the Broad Meadows ODW community is involved in a wide range of educational activities geared to prepare participants for the upcoming campaign. The goal is to develop global awareness, a sense of community, and democratic practices. Ron uses a series of semi-structured educational activities to help middle school students understand issues surrounding global inequality, poverty, and child labor. These activities build the foundation for the main event, evaluating project proposals submitted by various nongovernmental organizations (NGOs) and selecting a proposal to fund. The Child Labor Free Shopping Trip to the local mall—Shopping with a Conscience is the capstone general educational event.

CHAPTER 7: A YEAR IN THE LIFE PART 2: MAKING
THE PROJECT OF THE YEAR A REALITY

The second part of the year is the focus of chapter 7. After Thanksgiving the emphasis shifts to student-initiated fundraising and educational events that take place either at the school or in the Quincy community. Self-education continues, but its focus is the issues facing the youth in the project country. The group's relationship with the partner organization becomes a critical element in the self-education process. A focal point of the chapter is a case study of ODW's partnership with Goodweave and the unique educational opportunities this partnership provides for the students.

CHAPTER 8: PORTRAITS OF ODW ACTIVISTS

The chapter explores the experiences of seven students who were active in ODW. Three of the students started ODW organizations at their high schools after leaving Broad Meadows. One student is now a teacher who started and currently runs an ODW chapter at her middle school. This concluding chapter examines the impact of participation in ODW Broad Meadows on these students' lives.

Part I

THE KID'S CAMPAIGN TO BUILD A SCHOOL FOR IQBAL

Chapter 1

Prelude

From Pakistan to the USA

The children of Pakistan should have pens in their hands, not the tools of work. I am appealing to the people and the children of the US to not buy things made by the hands of little children; especially carpets.

—Iqbal Masih, age 12, former bonded child laborer

Punjab Province, Pakistan

Muridke in the Pakistani province of the Punjab has been described in various sources as a city, a town, a village, and even an industrial center. While there is little consensus on its designation, its location, 52 miles from Lahore, Pakistan's culture capital, is one of its major assets. Unfortunately, it shares Lahore's hot, arid climate. Temperatures can climb over 100°F in summer.

IQBAL'S STORY

In 1982, the year Iqbal Masih was born, the population of Muridke was approximately 108,000. Iqbal's father, Saif, was a day laborer who worked intermittently. His mother, Inayat, cleaned houses to provide for their seven children. The Masih family lived in conditions typical of Muridke's poor. They resided in a two-room, windowless house made of stone and made do without adequate food, clothing, or medical supplies.

Unlike the majority of Muridke's residents, the Masihs were Christian. (Masih is a common Christian name and means Messiah in Urdu.) In Muridke, as in the rest of Pakistan, Christians make up about 2.3% of the population and are often the subject of discrimination.

In 1986, Iqbal's older brother was to be married. It is customary for the groom's family to pay for part of the wedding and the Masihs would have been disgraced in this small Christian enclave if they did not comply with local tradition. Like most of Muridke's poor, the Masihs lived from hand to mouth. They had no savings to secure a bank loan. As a last resort, Saif Masih borrowed money from the owner of the local carpet factory. He promised the labor of his 4-year-old son, Iqbal, as collateral for the loan.

During the 1980s the *pesghi* system was legal in Pakistan. Under the pesghi system, employers advance money to workers who cannot leave until they repay the whole amount plus interest and/or expenses incurred. The owner could add the child's training, food, and the materials (s)he used to the initial debt. If the child made errors or rebelled, the owner could add fines. There was no formal contract and the owner kept the only records. Workers could not change jobs.

The Masih family borrowed 600 rupees, then the equivalent of $12.00. Iqbal became a debt bonded laborer at age four and was expected to weave carpets until the loan was repaid. He was required to work 12 hours a day, 6 days a week. He was picked up at 4:00 am and returned home at 7:00 pm. Each day, he received a half hour for lunch and was fed a meal of rice and lentils. The factory owner added the cost of lunch to the family's debt.

Initially, the owner promised Saif that his son would receive one rupee or two cents a day for his labor. However, when Iqbal arrived for work, the factory owner decided that the craft of carpet weaving was far too complicated for four-year-old Iqbal to learn quickly. He then told the family that Iqbal would spend his first year as an apprentice, learning the trade. Iqbal could not begin to pay back his father's debt until his second year of bondage.

Iqbal worked in a large room that fit 20 looms. Ventilation was minimal as the windows had to be sealed to protect the wool from insects. The children either squatted or sat on wooden platforms that were attached to a loom. Each child was provided with a paper map which showed where they should place the different colored wools. The child then knotted the wool and beat it down with a comb. He/she then repeated this process over and over throughout the 12-hour workday.

A trained weaver can make a four-by-six-foot carpet in six months. The factory foreman feared that the children would make errors, so he did not let them socialize or even speak. Children were hit on the head, neck, or back if they appeared to be lagging in their work. If the children resisted the work, they could be punished or tortured. This was Iqbal's plight and it is shared by millions of children throughout the world today (Kuklin, 1998).

CHILD LABOR

According to the International Labor Association (ILO), approximately 352 million children under the age of 18 are "economically active" worldwide. An estimated 211 million of these children are 5–14-year-olds and 141 million are 15–17-year-olds. One in six of these children can be classified as child laborers and, like Iqbal, are working under hazardous conditions (2002).

Of these 211 million children, 60% or 127 million work in Asia and the Pacific, 23% or 48 million in sub-Saharan Africa, 6% or 13.4 million in North Africa and the Middle East, and 8% or 17.4 million in Latin America and the Caribbean. Child labor does not only exist in the developing world, but occurs to a lesser extent in developed nations primarily in agriculture. In addition to carpet weaving, children work in mining, brick-making, agriculture, construction, tanneries, deep sea fishing, glass factories scavenging, and slate-making (2002).

At the 1999 International Labor Conference, 175 delegates from around the world adopted recommendation 190, which called for the elimination of the worst forms of child labor. These include slavery or practices similar to slavery, sale and trafficking of children, debt bondage, forced recruitment of children for the armed forces, child prostitution, pornography, drug trafficking, or hazardous work that is detrimental to a child-s health (ILO, 2004, pp. 44–46).

Children engaging in these hazardous types of labor are subject to injuries, pesticide poisoning, growth deficiencies, malnutrition, and long-term health problems such as cancer and respiratory disease. Child prostitutes often contract AIDS or other STDs.

Poverty is both a cause and a consequence of child labor in poor countries and communities. Many families living in extreme poverty rely upon the children's contributions to meet the family's basic needs for food and clothing. As there is limited access to education, health care, or other social services, many families lack options and become trapped in intergenerational poverty that is cyclical in nature. In addition, the AIDS epidemic has left many orphans who must work to survive.

Economic globalization exacerbates the situation. As multinational corporations expand, they seek the lowest labor costs. In order to compete for jobs, the governments of many poor countries ignore or intermittently enforce international child labor standards, although they have ratified international agreements.

CONDITIONS IN PAKISTAN

Pakistani children have worked alongside their parents in agriculture for 100 of years. However, they did not work outside of their families until the 1960s

when the government made a concerted effort to expand the country's industrial base. To compete in the global economy, manufacturers try to keep labor
costs low. In the carpet industry three to four children can be employed for
the cost of one adult and provide the manufacturer with a competitive edge
(Silvers, 1996).

It is difficult to estimate the number of child laborers currently working in
Pakistan. Sources vary and estimates range from 10 to 21 million child laborers.
According to the US Department of Labor, bricks, carpets, coal, glass, bangles,
leather, surgical instruments, and coffee are currently produced by children.

In Pakistan, the average annual household income is approximately
$421.00 and 35% of the population lives below the international poverty
line. An estimated 49.9% of the population can read and write; 63% of the
males and 35% of the women are literate. Dire poverty and limited educational opportunities make it difficult to break out of the cycle of poverty and
child labor. Despite laws prohibiting child labor, the local government has
done little to enforce the laws. In the late 1980s and early 1990s, the struggle
to eliminate the worst forms of child labor fell on Pakistani human rights
groups, such as the Pakistani Bonded Labor Liberation Front (BLLF).

Human Rights in Pakistan

The origins of the BLLF were rather serendipitous. According to Kuklin
(1998), in 1967, Eshan Ullah Khan, a middle class college student who
wanted to be a journalist, was walking down the streets of Lahore when he
came upon a crying man. He asked the man what was troubling him and the
man, Baba Kullan, introduced Khan to the plight of Pakistani debt-bonded
laborers. Kullan worked in a brick-making kiln. The owner of the kiln sold
Kullan and his two daughters, aged 11 and 13 years. The new owner and the
middleman raped both his girls. Kullan had escaped and was devastated.

Khan gathered a group of his friends and went to the police. Because of
the upper middle class status of the members of the student group, the police
were not able to ignore the situation and Kullan's daughters were returned to
him. The news of this event spread throughout the bonded labor community.

Other laborers began to contact Khan. He decided to take up the cause and
founded the Brick Kiln Laborers Liberation Front (BKLLF). They organized
demonstrations against bonded labor and provided the workers with legal
assistance. Khan supported this fledgling organization with money he made
as a journalist. He was arrested many times for his work with BKLLF and for
issues related to the freedom of the press. In 1982, Khan wrote an article that
claimed that biological warfare germs were being tested on brick kiln workers
in a controlled lab outside Lahore. As a consequence he spent six months in
Lahore Fort, a prison notorious for torture.

Bonded Labor Liberation Front

Despite these hardships, Khan continued his work. In 1988, he expanded the organization's base and formed the Bonded Labor Liberation Front (BLLF) that fought against different types of bonded labor. The BLLF had a legal and an educational field branch. Its legal work focused on changing legislation and court activity.

The BLLF campaigned against the *pesghi* system. This campaign was instrumental in the passage of two child labor laws: the 1991 Employment of Children Act that prohibited the use of child labor in hazardous occupations and the 1992 Bonded Labor Act that abolished indentured servitude—the *pesghi* system—and canceled all debts that the families owed to the factory owners.

Owners who violated the law and attempted to continue bondage could receive a minimum two-year jail term and stiff fines, that is, if local organizations enforced the law. In poor communities such as Muridke, public servants often depended upon bribes from factory owners to supplement their meager salaries. The government did little to enforce the law.

The BLLF played an important role in educating workers and informing them of their rights. They traveled around the country, held rallies, and distributed pamphlets, "The Charter of Freedom," which could be shared by those bonded laborers who could read. The BLLF offered legal services to workers to help secure their release.

APNA (Alternative) Schools

Another of the BLLF's major goals was to organize and educate bonded child laborers. Khan believed that change would come only through education and development that followed a democratic path. He felt that the children could play a vital role in eliminating child labor if they could become empowered through education and an understanding of democracy and human rights.

The BLLF opened 77 primary schools around the country for freed child laborers. The schools were called the APNA schools or our schools. They provided basic education and focused on literacy, health, and human rights and stressed the involvement of girls and women. The Freedom campus was established in Lahore. Its purpose was to help former bonded laborers understand their rights and help them to become self-organized so that they would not become bonded again. At a presentation in 1994, Khan said:

> Now thousands of children in the carpet industry are free. They are studying in our schools. We have schools without shelter ... under the tree in open grounds because we don't have resources. Only we have one blackboard, one table for the teacher. This is our school.

They are getting an education five hours a day and they are not working. But during their education, they are learning the rights of the child. They learn how to live ... how other children of the country are getting education and enduring their lives. This is our special awareness education. For these children live and fight for their lives and due to this awareness our children are very strong. They can speak. They can fight for their rights and never feel ashamed any more. (video of Iqbal's visit to Broad Meadows Middle School, 1994)

BLLF RESCUES IQBAL

Iqbal was unaware of outside efforts on behalf of child laborers. Like many bonded laborers, he was illiterate and had no access to the media. At age 8, he began to run away whenever he could. Once he ran to a police station and lodged a complaint. The officer promptly returned him to the factory, where he was severely beaten. By the time he turned ten, Iqbal had been working as a carpet weaver for six years. He earned 20 rupees, the equivalent of 40 cents a day. His family had taken out additional loans against his *pesghi*. He had incurred fines for his attempted escapes and other forms of resistance. His debt had grown from 600 rupees ($12.00) to 13,000 rupees ($260).

There are differing accounts of Iqbal's meeting and subsequent rescue by the BLLF. Factory owners were aware of the new laws and the BLLF. The owner of the carpet factory threatened Iqbal and the other workers and told them not to become involved or attend the local rally. Iqbal managed to escape and attend.

Remembering Iqbal on that day, Eshan Ullah Khan said, "He sat cowering in a corner, emaciated and wheezing like an old man. It was like he was trying to hide himself, to disappear, he was so frightened. But I felt that there was something in this boy, that he had a strong will" (in Kuklin, 1998, p. 56).

At the rally, Khan told the bonded laborers about the new law. He asked for volunteers to speak about their experiences. Iqbal, 3 feet 9 inches in height, rose and spoke out against the treatment he and the other children were subjected to at the carpet factory. Some sources indicate that after the rally Iqbal refused to return to the factory and that he received a certificate of freedom which he brought to the factory owner. Other sources say that Khan went to the owner and negotiated Iqbal's release, paying the owner with BLLF funds.

Khan needed Iqbal's mother's permission to bring him to the BLLF Freedom campus in Lahore. At first Inayat did not believe that Iqbal's debt had been canceled and was afraid that the family would be called on to repay it. Her husband had abandoned the family and they were barely able to subsist. Once she realized that Khan was telling the truth, she was torn. Like many parents living in abject poverty, she wanted her son to go to school, but she also needed help in supporting her seven children. She felt that Iqbal might be able to contribute in some other way. Khan understood and offered to provide the family with the money they would need to survive while Iqbal attended school.

Iqbal attended school at the Freedom campus and completed the four-year education program in just two years. During that time, he went to BLLF rallies, where he shared his experiences and recruited other youth. Again sources vary, indicating that he was instrumental in recruiting anywhere between 2,000 and 3,000 bonded child laborers.

He became president of the Children's wing of the BLLF. In November 1994, Khan took Iqbal to the International Labor Organization's conference in Stockholm, Sweden, where Iqbal told the story of his life as a bonded laborer in a carpet factory. He also visited Swedish schools. One month later Iqbal traveled to Boston to receive the Reebok Youth in Action award. Jennifer Margulis, who worked at Reebok, remembered her first encounter with Iqbal:

> When I first met Iqbal, he looked both younger and older than his 12 years. He was tiny, his growth stunted from years of malnutrition. His hands were leathery and criss-crossed with scars, his back hunched.

Iqbal asked the award's organizers if he could visit schools in the Boston area and meet children his own age. Reebok chose to send Iqbal to visit Broad Meadows Middle School because of its Human Rights curriculum and its history of youth activism. The encounter with Iqbal was eye opening for the American middle school students. He gave global inequality a human face and they were shocked to learn about the exploitation of children and youth around the world.

Chapter 2

Quincy, Massachusetts, USA

Teaching is the uncanny art of intellectual temptation.

—Jerome Bruner

Ron Adams was named Massachusetts state teacher of the year in 1991–1992. His former principal, Larry Taglieri, called him "a teacher super star." At 64, Mr. Adams retains his love of the kids and his enthusiasm for the classroom. However, he dislikes, even disclaims, the teacher superstar mantra. He feels that the school climate of the 1980s empowered teachers by allowing them to create innovative programs through work in interdisciplinary teams.

Teaching is not the typical career choice for "a kid from South Boston." However, his South Boston background aids his understanding of the students of Quincy, a white ethnic community that is predominantly working class and is becoming increasingly more diverse.

RON'S STORY

Ron's family crossed the Atlantic in the 19th century. His mother's family is from Ireland. His father's family is from Scotland. His grandmother snuck into the United States with a total of three dollars. She lied to the immigration officers at Ellis Island and said that she was coming over because her parents were here and had sent for her. She then moved to Boston.

His father's family moved from Scotland to England. They migrated to Canada where they stayed for a 100 years and then moved on to Boston. In the 1900s there were only three neighborhoods where the working class Irish (and Scots) could afford to live: South Boston, Dorchester, and Charlestown.

The Italian immigrants inhabited Boston's North End. Both of Ron's parents' families settled in South Boston and he was raised there. Ron's mother, Alice, was a stay-at-home mom. His father, Russell, was a professional musician, a drummer by trade.

Alice and Russell had two boys and two girls. Ron was the third child. The family lived in a three-room apartment, in a three decker. It was called this because there were three families on top of each other. Ron said, "We were probably below the poverty line, but we didn't know it." Neither of his parents went beyond the 8th grade in school. His older brother and sister went to South Boston High School. His mother wanted Ron to be the first in his family to attend college and decided that he should go to an "exam school," a college-bound specialty high school. Ron went to Boston Technical High School. He liked school but he went mostly to please his mother.

Boston Technical High School prepared Ron well. He won a scholarship to Northeastern University to study civil engineering. His guidance counselor recommended engineering because Ron's math SAT scores were very high. Nobody in Ron's orbit had experience with college or career selection, so he followed his guidance counselor's advice.

In his fourth year he realized that he had made a mistake and that engineering was not for him. He wanted to work with people and do something that helped others. He had always wanted to be a teacher, but initially, he was afraid that a teaching career lacked glamour, prestige, and adequate pay. Despite these qualms, Ron decided to follow his heart and transferred to the University of Massachusetts, Boston's teacher education program in English. He loved it.

Although he was first in his family to attend college, Ron received mixed messages from his parents. His mother supported and encouraged him, while his father was indifferent and skeptical. Russell had joined the Musician's Union at age 16 and worked as a member of house bands at clubs and at private functions. As technology changed, the DJ with the turntable replaced the live bands and the union went belly up. He lost his pension and his benefits. After paying dues for 50 years he had to work as a water meter reader and courier to survive.

Russell's life experiences led him to believe that the only way to advance was through inherited wealth or political connections. He repeatedly told Ron that he was going to end up working a "hard job" because the "working stiff" could never get ahead. Unlike his father, his friends from South Boston encouraged him. They took pride in the fact that somebody from the neighborhood would graduate from college.

At age 11, Ron had been secretly moved by JFK and the notion of "Camelot." The maxim "Ask not what your country can do for you. Ask what you can do for your country," resonated with him. He wanted to give back to the community and teach in the Boston Public Schools. His advisor at the University of Massachusetts, Boston, wanted him to see something different and sent him to Quincy, a suburb 7 miles south of the city limit to do his student teaching.

Ron began teaching at North Quincy High School. A teacher became pregnant at the rival Quincy High School and the department chair recommended Ron. He said, "It had been a long journey, but I finally felt like I was someplace where education mattered and there were like-minded people. I loved the Quincy public schools."

Two years later there were budget cuts and Ron was riffed. He was moved from high school to middle school. He was angry, but he had married Patricia Sullivan, a social worker, and their first son Ronald Patrick had arrived in 1975, so he decided to take a job at Atlantic Middle School and look for a high school position. Ironically, the move that he initially saw as a compromise based upon necessity provided the environment and structure conducive to his teaching goals. Patricia and Ron had two other sons, Michael Joseph in 1977 and Kevin Russell in 1983. Ron stayed at Middle School and grew more and more involved in the fledgling middle school movement with its student-centered pedagogy.

For Ron, the appeal of the middle school was the students. He became enchanted with the age group. He liked the idealism, curiosity, and energy of the young adolescents and believed that teachers could reach students at this age. The middle school students he worked with generally attended school every day, whereas at the high school level, he found that the students, teachers most needed to reach, cut class regularly or had already dropped out. Ron feels that middle school is the time that a teacher can inspire and motivate kids and get them to love learning because they are still at an age "when they don't know their limits and they are willing to try any assignment and believe that anything is possible."

Ron stayed at Atlantic Middle School for 4 years and then there were more budget cuts. He was transferred to Broad Meadows Middle School in 1983. When he walked through the front door at Broad Meadows, he saw a plaque on the right-hand side of the wall that said "Ask not what you can do for your country" and Ron thought to himself, "This is it."

Ron, like many teachers, entered the profession as a young idealist. He saw teaching as a chance to serve, to help youth, and to work for social justice and change for a better world. In order to develop a philosophy, pedagogy, and structure to work toward these ends, he needed to find a community and school culture that was compatible with these goals. Quincy, with its history of innovation and diversity, was an excellent fit.

THE QUINCY COMMUNITY

Quincy's unique history has influenced the direction of schooling in the community and is a source of pride for its residents. Quincy was the home of two US presidents, John Adams and John Quincy Adams, and the well-known American revolutionary John Hancock. It is also a city of firsts. It was the site of both the Iron Furnace that produced the first commercial iron in the United States and the granite railway, the country's first commercial railroad. Quincy was also the home of Howard Johnson and Dunkin Donuts. Francis W. Parker, who John Dewey called the Father of Progressive Education in America, was Quincy's first Superintendent of Schools.

Center of the Progressive Education Movement

In 1875, Parker was hired by the Quincy School Committee to reorganize the public schools. The Committee had been disappointed by the results of the students' end of year oral exams and believed a radical change was needed. The prevailing pedagogy of the era consisted of providing teachers with prescribed texts which the students committed to memory.

The school committee found that rote memorization and recitation produced a student body largely unable to use or transfer their knowledge to real-life situations or to other school-based learning situations for that matter. The majority of students knew the rules of grammar and spelling, but could not write a simple letter. They could read and answer questions from their school texts, but could not fluently read and/or recall information from unfamiliar texts at a similar reading level. When questioned about history most just regurgitated their texts. Many had difficulty using or applying math beyond the classroom setting.

Francis Parker, a former Colonel and school teacher, had just returned from Berlin where he studied the methodologies of Pestalozzi, Frobel, and Herbart and visited European schools that were experimenting with these new student-centered educational philosophies. He introduced an experiential, child-centered curriculum and pedagogy into the Quincy schools. He threw out the old texts and began a regime of in-service teacher training.

In Quincy, students learned by doing and Parker's emerging pedagogy became known as the "Quincy Method." In 1880, a school inspector from the Massachusetts State Board of Education visited the county schools and found that the students from Quincy did the best in the county in all of the fundamental subjects, except for Mathematics, where they ranked third. Parker's legacy lives on in Quincy and is a source of pride, especially for the members of Quincy's educational community (Nehring, 2009).

Quincy's Diversity

Quincy is also a city that is rich in its diversity. Its first inhabitants, the Massachusett, the Native American tribe, for which the state is named, lived in the area around Quincy Bay. Their numbers were decimated in 1617 due to an epidemic that most likely came from a visiting European ship. However, many of the survivors' ancestors reside in Quincy.

During the colonial period, the majority of the settlers were from England. They were joined by skilled glassworkers who arrived from Germany in the 1750s to work in the Quincy glassworks factory. They attempted to create a new planned community, Germantown. Ten years later the factory failed; however, many of the residents remained and the neighborhood has retained its name to the present day.

Quincy's shoreline gave it a natural advantage in the building of large ships. Thousands of people emigrated to Quincy to work in its shipyards. Quincy shipbuilding produced ships over 300 years from wood and sail, to steel and nuclear power. For example, Quincy's most famous shipyard, the Bethlehem Steel Fore River Shipyard, designed and constructed 100s of desperately needed warships in record time for the US Navy during World War II. The aircraft carrier USS Lexington, the battleship USS Massachusetts, the heavy cruiser USS Salem were all Quincy built, and are now floating museums.

The industries that developed as a consequence of Quincy's geography made it a magnet for a diverse mix of immigrants from the 1820s to the 1920s. The Irish were the first to come to Quincy and remain the city's largest ethnic group. The expanding granite industry stimulated immigration and urbanization. Immigrants, who were stonecutters by trade, gravitated to Quincy. These included Scots, Swedes, Finns, Norwegians, and Italians. During the 1800s, half of the working population was employed in the granite industry.

In addition to Italians, immigrants from southern and eastern Europe as well as the Middle East migrated to Quincy. These new Americans from Greece, Russia, Poland, Syria, and Lebanon found work in the quarries, factories, and the burgeoning shipbuilding industry (Quincy Historical Society, 2007).

Beginning in the 1980s, a new wave of immigrants, mostly of Asian ancestry, began to migrate to Quincy. This population has been increasing steadily. The US census reported 990 residents of Asian descent in 1980. By the 1990 census, there were 5,577 residents. The number more than doubled in the 2000 census at 13,546. As of the 2010 census, there are 22,174 residents of Asian ancestry or approximately 24% of the city's population. The majority are of Chinese ancestry, followed by immigrants from South East Asia, most notably Vietnam.

BECOMING A MIDDLE SCHOOL: TEAM AND DREAM

Ron Adams' educational outlook combined Quincy's tradition of educational innovation with his desire to create a welcoming tolerant environment for Quincy's newest residents. In 1981, Quincy public schools moved from the junior high school to the middle school model. The goal of the middle school movement was to "create schools that are developmentally appropriate and based upon the needs and characteristics young adolescents" (George & Alexander, 2003, p. 46).

Teachers no longer met as members of subject matter departments, but as interdisciplinary teams. English, Social Studies, Math, Science, and elective teachers who shared the same students met on a daily basis for 45 minutes to discuss students' progress and develop interdisciplinary curriculum that was student centered. They were also encouraged to develop additional electives that met once a week. According to the middle school concept, young adolescence was seen as a time for "purposeful exploration" (Jackson & Davis, p. 23).

Broad Meadows principal, Ann Marie Zukauskas, told the teachers to develop mini-courses where they could teach what they love and share their passion with the students. The teachers dubbed the model "Team and Dream."

The Human Rights Curriculum

Ron's team realized that the ethnic composition of the community was changing and believed that education was key to making a positive community transition. He said, "When the first Asian students came to our school, we started to see a little friction. They were living in the Germantown housing projects. Half of the students who attend Broad Meadows live in these low income housing projects. The projects went from 100% white to 90% white to 80% white and are becoming increasingly more Asian over time."

During the 1980s the majority of the new Asian students were in elementary school, but Ron's team knew that they would be coming to Broad Meadows as it was the feeder school for the projects. The staff decided to develop an interdisciplinary year-long Human Rights elective. They felt that if they began by looking at prejudice within Quincy the students would most likely get defensive and turn off. However, the teachers believed that if they began by looking at violations around the world, then moved to the United States as a whole, and ended with a focus on their local community, the students would be more willing to reflect and evaluate the situation in their own city and school. Ron explained:

> We decided that we would have a Human Rights curriculum in which we would study things far away that were definitely wrong, like Apartheid in South Africa.

We'd study that and the kids would say "That's wrong. That's not fair." Then we would study something in the U.S like the Civil Rights Movement, Ruby Bridges for example and the kids would say, "That is wrong. That is not fair."

Gradually we hoped to move the curriculum to our own community, and say: "Well what about someone who moves here from another country and they don't know how to speak English perfectly? What if we make fun of them because they talk differently? Oh, that's wrong, that's not fair." So, by starting far away with clear examples, we thought that we could move gradually to questioning ourselves. "Are we acting like that in any way? Are we in any way acting racist?"

The 8th-grade Human Rights elective was content driven. The teachers located short nonfiction reading selections on topics such as apartheid in South Africa, the troubles in Northern Ireland, or other current examples of Human Rights violations.

The Human Rights elective was such a success that Ron and his teammate Donna Willoughby, the 7th-grade Social Studies teacher, decided to work collaboratively to integrate Human Rights into the 7th-grade curriculum. However, while the readings generated great discussion, the discussions tended to stay within the classroom. The students were not using their newly acquired knowledge to take action in the real world.

The teachers decided to try to locate guest speakers who were experts in the topics they were studying to make the topics really come alive. They started to contact organizations that were interested in working with the schools. Facing History and Amnesty International had guest speaker programs and curriculum materials on relevant topics. Facing History sent a Catholic priest from Northern Ireland who spoke about the troubles there and a Holocaust survivor who shared his story and spoke about genocide. Amnesty International provided an activist who had recently returned from Central America where he had helped to monitor elections.

As the curriculum evolved, each Friday in Social Studies the students would study content in Donna's class. In English class, Ron had the students study two texts of ideal behavior, the UN Declaration of Human Rights and the Bill of Rights of the US Constitution. He used the ideals set forth in these documents as a baseline and would ask the students to compare global, national, and local realities to these ideals.

Students were required to identify an issue that they found unfair and write a business letter protesting this injustice. The letter could be to anyone, an elected official, a person in their church, a friend. In the first paragraph they had to identify the human rights violation and in the second paragraph they had to ask the recipient to join them in action. It could be an action that the teachers had already introduced or a new action that the student came up with. Ron required that they send in the letters and bring in the responses to the class. He said:

This was my first exposure to challenging students to do something in the real world about human rights. I thought business letters were the safest way for kids to raise their voices. A lot of the kids are shy ... so their fragile idealistic voices are put down on paper. ... Those letters were phenomenal.

Activism became an integral part of both the 7th-grade interdisciplinary curriculum and the 8th-grade Human Rights elective. Students could suggest issues that they heard about that troubled them, thus adding to the curriculum. Most importantly, they decided which issues they wanted to pursue. Taking action became a matter of choice and conscience.

LOCAL ACTIVISM

School Safety

The letters resulted in several activist campaigns and began with a focus upon local grievances. Several students were upset because drivers were ignoring the speed limit on the street most had to cross to get to school. They felt unsafe crossing the street. One of the students wrote to the mayor and eventually met with him. A traffic officer was sent to the corner to collect data on the car speeds. He found that the motorists were going 48 miles an hour. (The speed limit was 30 miles per hour.) The city put in radar traps to ensure that drivers drove at the speed limit. This victory seemed monumental to the middle schoolers. They were amazed that that they could influence adults to take action.

Educating Against Drunk Driving

Several months later, a drunk driver speeding down that same street at night killed a Broad Meadows Middle School student, his mother, his brother, and his sister. Lisa, a 7th grader in Ron's English class, was outraged by this accident. Encouraged by her classmate's success, she decided to take action. She felt that tragedies such as this could be avoided if education about the consequences of drunk driving began in middle school.

Lisa wrote a letter to Governor Michael Dukakis advocating this curriculum change. To her surprise the governor responded. He asked her to bring ten of her classmates, her teacher, and the principal to meet with him in Boston. They decided that the students should develop a middle school curriculum. The students created a 56-page curriculum which they called, "Not me, I can Handle It." The curriculum featured interviews that the students conducted with law enforcement, elected leaders, rehabilitation administrators, and victims of drunk driving. Governor Dukakis wrote the introduction. The curriculum was bound and distributed to middle schools throughout the state.

The result of the students' second and bigger victory spread throughout the community. The students began to realize that they could make their voices heard. This nascent sense of empowerment led to bigger and more ambitious activist campaigns.

THE BEGINNINGS OF GLOBAL ACTIVISM

The Campaign to Free Nafije Zendeli

In fall 1989, CBS affiliate, Boston 7, WNEV-17, partnered with Amnesty International to highlight Amnesty's Prisoners of Conscience Campaign. The network decided to involve young adolescents by introducing Prisoners of Conscience on Ready to Go (RTG), a live, weekday morning news broadcast geared to a middle school audience. A member of the RTG staff researched schools in the greater Boston area to find a partner middle school and learned about the Broad Meadows Human Rights program through Amnesty International.

RTG decided to feature Amnesty Prisoner of Conscience, Nafije Zendeli, on its show. Nafije was a 17-year-old student of Albanian descent who lived in the former Yugoslavia. Nafije and other Albanian students wanted classes taught in their own language. The students formed a group, the "Freedom Society," to protect the rights of Albanians in Yugoslavia. The group organized a peaceful demonstration against a new law that limited access to education in the Albanian language on October 4, 1988. Nafije was arrested and sentenced to 4 years in prison for her role in the protest.

Building upon prior letter writing campaigns, Channel 7 invited all of the Broad Meadows students to engage in a Letters of Conscience Week from November 13 to 17, 1989. It began with a Kick off Assembly in which the week's activities were explained. The students were asked to write letters to the Yugoslavian Ambassador requesting freedom for Nafije Zendeli in their Language Arts classes. They were also asked to design symbolic chains. On Friday, Chain Day, students would wear their symbolic chains to a special assembly with the RTG cast. Tina Youthers, a human rights activist and an actor on the TV show Family Ties, appeared at the assembly to thank the students and collect the 350 letters that would be delivered to an appropriate Yugoslavian official.

The Chain Day Assembly was filmed and broadcast on RTG the following week. Two Broad Meadows students, Julie Lai and Shari Brennan, were selected to appear on the show and ask viewers to write a letter. As a result of

Broad Meadows campaign and the broadcast of the Chain Day Assembly, the
network received a total of 3,500 letters from the Greater Boston area. The
TV station contacted Massachusetts Senator John Kerry, who was serving on
the Foreign Relations Committee, to see if he could arrange for representatives of Broad Meadows and RTG to deliver the letters and meet with the
Yugoslavian Ambassador.

The TV station paid for Shari and Julie, the hosts of the TV program, a
camera crew, and teacher chaperone (Ron Adams) to fly to Washington, DC
for the meeting. When they arrived in Washington, DC, Senator Kerry met
them on the steps of the Capitol and told them that Nafije Zendeli had been
freed.

While the Zendeli Campaign was not student initiated, it provided Broad
Meadows' students and teachers an opportunity to partner with external
organizations, network TV, and Amnesty International and demonstrated to
the students that they could make a difference through participation. It also
provided Ron with media and political connections that he could use to help
his students in future campaigns.

The Campaign to Free Nafije Zendeli received a Multicultural Recogni-
tion Award for Connections Abroad from the Massachusetts State Board of
Education. The students were honored at a ceremony at the JFK Library in
Boston on May 10, 1991. In addition, Ron was one of eleven teachers in
New England selected to receive the World of Difference award for fostering
student awareness.

PRESERVING LOCAL HISTORY

The USS Salem: The Campaign to Build
a Museum of Quincy's History

During the 1988–1989 school year, as part of the team's interdisciplinary study of the industrial revolution, the 7th grade took a trip to Lowell,
Massachusetts, to visit the mill museum. One of the 7th graders Margaret
(who is currently a member of the Quincy City Council) felt that it was
unfair that Lowell had a museum and Quincy did not. She felt that Quincy's
maritime history merited a museum. Margaret started writing letters, dozens
of letters, to local and state officials asking them to develop a shipbuilding
museum that would tell the history of the ships and shipbuilders of the Fore
River Ship Yard in Quincy.

Margaret began to get responses from local and state officials and the
campaign to build a shipbuilding museum took off. It became a class project
that spread across the entire 7th grade. Then it snowballed and the 6th and

8th graders joined in and it became a school-wide project. The students wanted the US Navy to donate a ship built in Quincy that would become a living floating ship museum that would be docked at the Quincy shipyard.

The students launched a petition drive and succeeded in getting all 12 state senators from New England to endorse the Quincy Museum. Margaret spoke before the City Council asking for their support. The Mayor, James Sheets, a former History professor at Quincy College, provided the leadership and became a point person for the campaign. The City Council unanimously endorsed the idea and helped to organize a committee that consisted of a volunteer staff to develop a plan for a museum. Three years later, the navy donated the USS Salem to Quincy as the museum's centerpiece. The ship was towed by tugboats from Philadelphia to Quincy. The students and their former teacher were invited to accompany the boat on its journey.

While obtaining the ship was the focus of the campaign, the students began to wonder about the actual people who were involved; the sailors who manned the ship during the war and the people who were involved in building the ships. With Ron's help and encouragement, the twenty students who were most actively involved started an oral history project. They initially located sailors and the men who had worked in the shipyards. Their work with the men raised the question of the women's role in the shipbuilding industry and another project developed, which the students' dubbed the Winnie the Welder Oral History Project.

For both projects the students collected tools, photographs, and conducted and transcribed oral histories. The students did not want to record the interviews with cheap video equipment, so Ron suggested that the students contact the local cable company to see if they could use their equipment. Representatives from the company agreed to come to the school and train the students on how to use professional grade equipment. The interviews took place at the school, in people's homes, and at nursing homes.

When the representatives of the local cable company saw some of the raw footage, they decided to make a documentary about the shipyard, using the shipbuilder's voices. They brought ten of the original interviewees to the studio and recorded new interviews. The Broad Meadows students conducted the interviews on camera and were involved in the editing process. The final documentary was 30 minutes in length and was called Quincy Pride: Quincy Shipbuilding. It was shown regularly on the local cable station for years.

RON'S EVOLVING PHILOSOPHY AND PRACTICE

As stated in the introduction, situated learning theory posits that humans shape and are shaped by participation in activities in the communities and institutions they are involved with on a regular basis. Ron's views of learning, pedagogy, and his identity as an educator were formed by his participation in professional communities with his colleagues and the classroom and informal communities with his students. The professional communities that exerted the most influence were the middle school interdisciplinary team at Broad Meadows, an intensive Leadership Academy offered by the state of Massachusetts, and his collaboration with Social Studies teachers Donna Willoughby and Eileen Sadof.

During the late 1980s and early 1990s when the middle school philosophy was at its height, English educators such as Nanci Atwell and Harvey Daniels were calling for student voice and choice in reading and assignment selections. Although Ron was an English teacher, he was also involved with debates in the Social Studies educational community.

During the summer of 1992, the state of Massachusetts offered an intensive Teacher Leadership Academy. It was sponsored by Harvard and the University of Massachusetts and met on the Harvard campus for five weeks in the summer and then once a month throughout the school year. Ron was one of 125 teachers from five different disciplines selected to attend.

The academy differed from other professional development opportunities as no outside speakers were brought in to train the teachers. The teachers were put into teams to develop curriculum. Because Ron had worked on the Human Rights curriculum he was asked to join the Social Studies group instead of the English group. Ron described the summer academy as a "freeing experience."

During their discussions, one of the teachers said that one of the biggest goals in Social Studies education is to teach students to become active citizens and to use history to deliberate and make decisions. However, she felt that this rarely went on and that in most classes, history was simply learning information about the past.

In the spirit of John Dewey, she posed the questions: When do you do democracy? When do you prepare students to become active citizens who deliberate and vote? If there is no democracy in the classroom how do you expect them to know how to debate, vote, and make informed decisions. These ideas resonated with Ron given his experiences with student-initiated campaigns and projects that evolved from the Human Rights curriculum. The interplay between participation in professional communities and reflection upon what he experienced in the classroom led Ron to experiment and take risks in the classroom.

Ron found that some of the topics that they introduced in the 8th-grade Human Rights elective and the 7th-grade interdisciplinary Fridays generated so much interest that the students wanted to continue the discussion during the next week. He decided to use the students' input and interest as a way to make the curriculum more meaningful.

On current events Fridays, Ron reserved 10 minutes out of his 55-minute period for student voice. He allowed the students input as to the way the Friday classes would progress. He said:

> I called it, SAVE ROOM FOR THE STUDENT VOICE. I trained myself to stop and ask them what they thought. I told them that I wanted to hear their ideas. At first they were skeptical. They would wait and watch and it would be silent.
>
> I became determined not to fill the silence with my voice. I would cross my hands and lean against the wall and wait. All of a sudden they started to realize … this guy is serious. He really wants to hear what we have to say. The comments that came out of the silences were deeper and better…. I built more of this into the classroom. The classes became much more exciting. I just loved the energy.

According to Ron the goal was not to have students control the curriculum but to let students have input, so that teachers and students could become a community learning together and deciding where they could go next. The students often became so excited about an issue that they did not want to wait an entire week to develop an action campaign and the project began to extend beyond the classroom. A new structure emerged wherein a core group of interested students requested an after school meeting and the campaign was opened to the entire 7th grade. Generally a dozen or more students would show for the meeting and they would take on the leadership roles.

Ron let the students have a say in how the meetings and current events Friday classes would be run. The students were allowed to make five rules and then vote. Generally, the students would come up with rules along the following lines, with a little prodding from Mr. Adams.

Everyone's comments are welcome, but you can only have one speaker at a time.
You can't cut anybody off
Everybody has a responsibility to speak
You can pass if you want
Nobody can criticize or mock what you say.
Don't abuse or hurt feelings.

Ron believes that in order for democratic practice to work whether in a classroom or at a before- or an after school program meeting the teacher/facilitator has to create a safe space where the students feel free to express themselves. In the classroom, in addition to discussion, journaling became an integral part of his practice so that students who remained shy about speaking up still had an opportunity to express themselves. He said:

> Students had so much energy during the Friday discussions and wanted to know more and do something about it and that was part of our design you know, make

the subject come alive, bring it home and never leave students with a sense of helplessness or hopelessness. Always provide them with some way to express their anger in positive action. Whatever the request, we tried, as teachers to support it and make it happen. We wanted them to feel like they could be part of a solution and not just part of an audience who discovers the injustice.

When Iqbal asked Reebok if he could meet students his own age on his visit to Boston, they were looking for a school where students would be likely to take action. The Boston branch of Amnesty International recommended Broad Meadows Middle School because of its Human Rights Program, its participation in the Zendeli Campaign, and its reputation for student-initiated activism.

CONCLUSION

Through participation in professional learning communities, Ron became familiar with the debates surrounding student-centered democratic pedagogy. He spoke about creating classes that resembled learning communities. However, classrooms are typically hierarchically structured spaces where the teacher is in charge. Ron wanted to create a safe space where students have input and feel free to express ideas while at the same time maintain order and provide the structure needed for meaningful learning to take place. To accomplish this goal he needed to experiment and refine his ideas about youth participation.

Youth participation also referred to as youth voice, youth empowerment, and youth engagement has been advanced as a component of student-centered pedagogy since the time of John Dewey (Kohn, 1993). In this analysis, youth participation is defined as "the constellation of activities that empower adolescents to take part in and influence decision making that affects their lives and to take action on issues that they care about" (O'Donoghue, Kirshner, & Mc Laughlin, 2002, p. 16). Youth participation was officially recognized as a basic right in September 1990 when the United Nations Convention on the Rights of the Child was ratified by 191 nations.

The Human Rights curriculum was Ron's first experiment with youth participation and democratic pedagogy. During this time period, research and experimentation with youth participation was taking place in English and Social Studies educational settings. In English, the focus was upon curriculum choices. Teachers and researchers advocated for more student choice of book selections and assignments (Atwell, 1987; Daniels, 1994). Social Studies researchers and educators concerned about the schools' civic mission advocated "doing democracy" through the incorporation of democratic practice, deliberative discussion, and civic engagement (Parker, 2003). Ron drew from his experience with the Human Rights curriculum and ideas in both disciplinary pedagogies in developing and refining his approach to teaching and learning.

Research indicates that effective and meaningful student participation requires institutional support systems (Barber, 2007). Harry Shier (2001, 2006) developed the Pathways to Participation matrix, a heuristic device that can be used to gauge increasing levels of youth participation in formal and informal educational settings.

Five levels of participation have been identified. At the most basic level, Level 1 youth are listened to. This is followed by adults actively supporting youth in expressing their views, Level 2. At Level 3, youth's views are taken into account when decisions are made. Youth become involved in the decision-making processes at Level 4. During the final stage, Level 5, youth share power and responsibility for decision making (2001, p. 108). According to Shier, youth participation increases when there are openings at the institutional level, opportunities for the teachers to obtain the necessary resources and support, and an agreed upon policy that allows student participation to lead to empowerment that becomes a part of the school culture.

At Broad Meadows, the structural shift from the junior high school to middle school organization coupled with strong administrative support for student-centered elements of the middle school concept provided the opening for greater youth participation. By endorsing the notion of exploration within coursework and through electives, student choice became a part of the school culture.

Restructuring from a departmental to team-based organization, with daily joint prep time and weekly team meetings, provided teachers with the opportunity, and one of the most critical resources, time, to reflect and develop innovative programs. Once the institutional structures and supports were in place Ron and his colleagues took off. They found outside organizations to provide innovative curriculum and training. Ron and his counterparts in Social Studies forged ongoing relationships with their curriculum providers, Facing History and Amnesty International.

Ron began his experiment with student voice at Level 2 on Shier's matrix. His goal at that point was to support his students in expressing their views. The student-selected business letter about an issue of conscience became a focal point for student self-expression and this activity became a requirement for his course. He also encouraged the expressions of students' views in classroom discussions and guided students in creating classroom rules that would create a safe space for this type of self-expression. He also incorporated choices in book selections and class assignments.

While Ron was willing to support student expression and take student views into account, he realized that for students to learn to practice democracy and develop a sense of agency and civic efficacy, they needed to learn to express their views and have them taken into account in the world outside of the school. He began to develop mechanisms (before and after school meetings) and provide support (mentoring and supplies) so that student-initiated activist campaigns could take place. He was backed in this work by his principal and this support allowed him to move the program to the third level of participation.

Once the mechanisms were in place, Ron began to involve the students in the decision-making processes of the various after school campaigns (Level 4). Democratic procedures were put in place that enhanced student discussion of campaign strategies. They took turns running meetings and voted on key issues that determined the events and progress of the various campaigns. With Ron's assistance they researched and wrote speeches that they presented to local officials and conducted oral histories for projects that they had initiated.

Student successes built upon one another and were publicized in the local press. The school developed a reputation in Quincy for youth activism. Recognition of student achievements led to increased administrative support for civic activism. It became part of the culture of the school. Encouraged by the program's successes, Ron integrated more democratic practice into his classes and the after school campaigns and became committed to involving students in the decision-making processes. He was ready to move to the next level of commitment: sharing power and responsibility in an after school campaign (Level 5) when Iqbal arrived at Broad Meadows.

The Broad Meadows students were also prepared. They were accustomed to democratic classroom practice and had been encouraged to express themselves and take action. They were proud of their school's history and reputation as an activist school and familiar with the successes of students who had come before them. Teachers had been empowered by the team structure and an environment where they were respected and encouraged to experiment. They, in turn, empowered their students.

Chapter 3

The Kid's Campaign to
Build a School for Iqbal

Iqbal's dream was for all children to be free and in a school. A bullet can't kill a dream.

—Amanda, 7th grader, Broad Meadows Middle School

IQBAL'S VISIT TO BROAD MEADOWS

On December 2, 1994, Iqbal Masih visited Broad Meadows Middle School. He was accompanied by Ehsan Ullah Khan, the president of the BLLF, Paula Van Gelder of the Reebok Foundation, and an Urdu/English translator from Boston University. He spent the day, spoke at different classes, and went to lunch with the students.

A video of the day shows a small, frail-looking boy about the size of a 7-year-old, with scars on hands and face, and big sad eyes. He is sitting in a desk in front of the sink in room 109, Ron Adams' room, an old science lab converted into an English classroom. On the chalkboard behind him, it says "Quincy, Mass. USA Welcomes Iqbal Masih 'Youth in Action.'" Middle school students are seated in a semicircle four rows thick around the desk.

Iqbal begins to speak. His voice is high pitched like a child's, but as he talks, it becomes apparent that he is a young man with a mission. His manner is determined. He is a youth addressing his peers. He wants their understanding and help. He says: "I am Iqbal. I was a working child. When I was working, the factory owners used to take me early every morning from my house, at 4:00 am and we had to work up to 6:00 or 7:00 at night."

He signals to the person sitting behind him. He hands Iqbal a plastic bag filled with props, the tools of the carpet trade. Iqbal picks up a foot-long metal instrument that consists of a handle with a head of spiked prongs and says, "This is what they used to hit us." When he demonstrates the movement, he is at Broad Meadows, yet at the same time faraway reliving the experience. "This is the thing that they used to beat up little children. They used to hit us on the head or the back at times. We would have lots of cuts."

Iqbal then picks another metal tool shaped like a small sickle. "This is the tool we used for work. It is very fast. It cut our fingers. But those people (the factory owners), did not take us to doctors. They suggested we put our fingers in hot oil."

Then his anger erupts:

> They (the owners) used to have torture cells. (If you protested or ran away …) They would put you in these torture cells. They used to tie our hands and feet… sometimes they would tie us upside down on the wall. Sometimes a child had to stay in the torture cells for three days and he was not given anything to eat or drink. Sometimes children used to get very sick and they used to just die. We were scared. They would say if we talked about it, they would put us in the room or throw us in hot oil.

Iqbal speaks in Urdu, through an interpreter. There are many breaks in the dialogue, yet there is total silence in the room; a silence uncharacteristic of 7th graders. During the question and answer session the Broad Meadows students pour out the questions that baffle them as the two worlds collide.

Did you have friends?
Did you ever get to play sports?
Did you ever get to play?
Did you see get to see your family?
Did you tell your parents about the torture?
Why didn't they do anything?
Iqbal tries to explain:

> My parents knew about the torture but they couldn't do anything. Whenever they used to complain the factory owners had some kind of hit man who would come and beat them up. He would threaten and harass them and say that they would tell the police that they stole something. … The poor can' do anything because rich people influence the court, the judiciary, and the police, so they (the poor) are just helpless. … So it is very easy for the owners to kill somebody and for them to give harm to someone.

A Broad Meadows student raises his hand and asks, "Are you scared?"
Iqbal replies, "I am not afraid of the situation anymore. On the contrary, I've gotten a lot of confirmations from the BLLF. I've been to Sweden and

now here. So the carpet industry people are afraid of me and my fellow children."

Ron Adams asks, "Are there still children working in the factory where you worked?"

Iqbal replies, "Yes, they have brought other children to replace those who are free ... I want you to help me and kids like me."

At lunch the kids gathered around Iqbal and went with him to recess. They brought him little gifts. Mr. Adams recalled, "It was spontaneous. They brought him pieces of their own childhoods as if they were trying to give him back what had been taken away."

Amanda, one of the Broad Meadows students, said:

It was funny. We gave him sticks of gum, and he would smack it. He loved gum. I remember learning about the things that he really liked. We made sure that we got him all of the things he liked and gave him a backpack full.

During last class of the day, the students gave him notes. Iqbal turned to them and through his translator he said,

I want to thank you for the wonderful day. When I came to America, I wasn't sure that I was going to like American kids. I was told by the rug manufacturers that Americans are devils. They have horns and tails. It was the Americans who buy carpets and the Americans make the Pakistanis make these rugs. The factory owners told us that we were the victims of the American devil. You are more like angels than devils and I am very relieved.

After Iqbal left, Ron asked the students to write in their journals. He said that the students' initial reaction to meeting Iqbal was rage. They couldn't believe that adults could do that to children. They had believed that slavery had been abolished by Abraham Lincoln and were confused and angry to learn that children still lived in bondage today.

The Tuesday following Iqbal's meeting at Broad Meadows, he received the Reebok Youth in Action Award and returned to Pakistan. The Broad Meadows students came up with an action plan. They decided to write business letters to people in power, protesting child labor. The students wrote more than 600 letters to political figures such as Prime Minister Benazir Bhutto of Pakistan and Massachusetts Senators John Kerry and Edward Kennedy.

They also decided to contact local carpet stores to find out if they sold rugs made by children. In addition, they voted to develop a time capsule. They wanted to do research and collect articles about child labor all over the world so that in 50 years, after child labor had been eradicated, people would know what went on.

Five months after his visit, on Easter Sunday, April 16, 1995, Iqbal was riding a bicycle to his grandmother's house and he was shot and killed. Ehsan Ullah Khan said that Iqbal had received death threats and claimed that the Carpet Manufacturers Association was behind the murder. His allegations were never investigated and the case remains unsolved. When the Broad Meadows Middle School students learned of Iqbal's death they were devastated and a letter writing campaign no longer seemed to be enough.

STUDENT VOICES: AMANDA

Amanda moved around a lot as a child. She was born on a Navy Base in Bremerton, Washington. Her family moved to Oregon after her dad got out of the Navy and they lived in Portland, Saint John's, and Scappoose. Her parents got divorced when she was 7. Amanda's father remarried a woman from Massachusetts. Her dad and stepmom decided to move to Quincy and bring Amanda with them. She was 12.

When Amanda entered 7th grade at Broad Meadows Middle School, she felt lost and confused. She didn't know who she was. Looking back, at age 29, Amanda said, "I would sit at the back of the room, I always sat at the back. I always listened and took notes and I would doodle, but I never raised my hand. I barely talked to anyone."

Amanda has vivid memories of Iqbal's visit. They were studying the Industrial Revolution and the stories of the girls who worked in the wool mill. Then the teachers announced that there was going to be a change of plan and they would be studying about what was going on in the world today to kids in other countries. The teachers shared Iqbal's story and prepared the students to be sensitive to differences, like size and childhood experiences.

Despite the preparation Amanda was shocked when Iqbal entered the classroom. She said:

When he walked in I was surprised ... because Mr. Adams had said "short," and I was thinking like the shortest kid in my class. ... And then watching him sit down and his feet would swing off of the chairs that our knees were hitting. ... But I was in awe. ... He was such a great speaker ... even for us not knowing the language. When he spoke you were captivated by his energy and his little voice. You could tell that he was serious and how much it really meant to him. ... I remember, I was thinking about how upset I was about how my life had turned out. ... But I had a home, food, clothes. Even with all the traumatic things that have happened, I had the opportunity to play and the right to go to school. I remember watching and listening and feeling very sad and then very angry ... like this is so wrong.

After Iqbal left, Amanda became one of the leaders of the letter writing campaign. She learned about Iqbal's death on April 15, 1995, the Sunday before the first day of Spring break.

Ron learned of Iqbal's death the same evening. He was upset about Iqbal and concerned about his students' reactions. He said, "I didn't want the kids to think this is what happens when a kid speaks out. ... He gets killed. I didn't want this to be the Human Rights lesson the students learned." Since the school was on Spring break he thought that he would have time to think of a way to handle this.

However, the next day, Monday, Ron received a phone call at home from the principal, Anne Marie Zukauskas. She said that she had received a call from a neighbor who lived by the school. The neighbor told her that there were dozens of kids hanging around the flagpole acting suspiciously. She wanted to know if Ron thought this could be related to Iqbal's death and asked him to meet her at the school.

Anne Marie arrived at Broad Meadows first. She found approximately 40 kids outside. When Ron arrived, she was deep in discussion with the students. Many had their heads down and some were crying. Anne Marie decided to open up the school and they all went into a classroom. They held a little memorial service and let the students vent. The middle school students had never known anyone who had been murdered. They didn't want Iqbal's dreams to die with him. Ron said:

I was deeply moved by the students' voices, I wanted to empower kids. I decided that I wasn't going to come up with anything. I wanted to give everybody a choice. So I gave them each a piece of paper and said, come back tomorrow at the same time and write your suggestions on the paper.

Amanda remembers:

Teachers and students met at BMMS. We talked about how amazing Iqbal was ... intelligent, funny committed. Even with the language barrier there was a connection between the peers. It was a time of reflection and a reality check for us kids that the issues presented to us by Iqbal were real ... and it just became a challenge for us to carry because it felt like the children in Pakistan were not protected enough for the fight. Then the brainstorming started as we filled our journals with emotion, after everyone left.

The majority of the students returned the next day. Word got out about the meeting and a reporter from the Boston Globe showed up at the school and asked to join them. Ron facilitated the meeting. He first asked the students how they wanted to share their ideas and they voted. They decided that

Mr. Adams would read their ideas anonymously. One of the ideas was to build a school in Iqbal's memory. Three different students who didn't know each other came up with this idea independently. The students discussed all the ideas and then they voted again. They decided to build a school in Iqbal's memory. Ron said:

> My mind started racing and I became numb with paralysis, I didn't want them to fail. My mind raced to the practical. Don't ask kids to come up with an idea unless it can be a success. Then, I decided I wasn't going to judge … so I handed out another piece of paper and said … you have to come up with a series of steps and show me how you are going to do this. We met the next day.

STUDENT VOICES: JEN

Jen is Quincy born and bred. She is one of two children. Her sister is three and a half years her junior. Jen's father is a mailroom operator. Her mom worked as a nurse's assistant in a Senior Citizen's home in Dorchester when Jen began working on the campaign.

Although Jen always lived in Quincy, her family moved around a lot within the city borders. Jen attended three different elementary schools. So when Amanda moved in from Oregon, Jen was sympathetic. She knew what it felt like to be the new kid and befriended her. At 29, Jen can remember Iqbal's visit "like it was yesterday." She said,

> When I met Iqbal, it was a no brainer. … It was like, I have to do something. I remember him walking into the classroom … and he was so small and … like even his hands … were so undeveloped. At that time I didn't know what malnourishment was and he was just stunted.

Jen was at a family friend's house when Iqbal got shot. She saw it on the news and called Amanda. She couldn't believe it and neither of them knew what to do and they ended up going over to the school the next day.

After the second meeting with Mr. Adams, a group of students including Jen and Amanda met and drew up a list of things they wanted to do. The core group of students was all in Ron's 7th-grade English class and had been practicing democracy in his class since September. They asked Mr. Adams to serve as an advisor for their campaign to build a school in Iqbal's memory. They voted on a meeting day, Fridays after school, as there were no club or sports meetings on that day.

As an advisor in a more informal setting, Ron was able to take his philosophy of youth participation and democratic citizenship education to the next level. He developed a youth-adult partnership wherein the students shared in the power and responsibility for decision making. Students came up with the ideas that they discussed and debated. Ron and other adults helped them to put these ideas into practice by providing resources and contacts or training in skills they needed to further their goals as activists on the campaign. The principal gave them her full support. Amanda recalled "Mr. Adams would help keep us on track, but if we came up with an idea he would say, 'How do you want to do this?' And then he would let us brainstorm and help us."

The students decided upon a kick-off event, a memorial service for Iqbal. A core group of activists climbed onstage and lit candles in the darkened auditorium and there was a moment of silence for Iqbal Masih. Once the lights turned back on, the students announced their plan to build a school for Iqbal and The Kid's Campaign was officially launched. Then shy Amanda, who never spoke up in class, announced to the entire Broad Meadows community, "Iqbal's dream was for all children to be free and in a school. A bullet can't kill a dream."

The students also decided to reach out to other students at other schools. Jen said: "We decided to ask for $12.00 because we figured it was symbolic. ... He was twelve when we met him, twelve when he died and he was sold for $12.00." Since there were about 24 students in a class, each student needed to contribute 50 cents to meet the goal. Student volunteers visited local Quincy Schools, both public and private, and made presentations about the campaign and asked for contributions. Mr. Adams served as mentor and editor, training the students in the art of writing and public speaking. Amanda said:

> Mr. Adams was really good at having us prepare as far as writing it down and making sure that our message was being heard. But he never made us practice a lot. The way that he went about it ... he didn't make it a job. So it wasn't boring for us, ever. He always had words of encouragement.
>
> If we had a speech, we would sit after school a couple of days a week and write down what we thought and talk about how we wanted it to come across and then we would have him edit a little bit .... But he always kept it in our words. He kept it real. ... And I think, in his mind too having our words on that paper and being comfortable with what we were saying was really what mattered.

The Broad Meadows students were not the only group in the Boston area moved to action by Iqbal's untimely death. The Boston Human Rights community was deeply shaken as well. They chose to dedicate their 7th annual Human Rights Festival to Iqbal Masih. The event, the Back Bay Festival, was held on April 27th and featured musical performances and speeches by Human Rights activists. Broad Meadows Middle School students were invited to speak and Amanda volunteered to represent them. She said:

It was a huge concert … all different local rock bands. It was a way to raise money for different causes and inform people about what was going on in the world. They would have speakers between bands and sets. There were like 2,000 people. I remember getting up there and boy, I was so nervous. I looked down the street and there was no pavement. There were people everywhere and I said, "Hey, I want to let everybody know that it takes a lot of guts to get up here ... so could I have your attention please." Then I spoke. I don't remember what I said. When I got down everyone was applauding.

When Rick Roth, festival organizer and coordinator for the Somerville/ Arlington chapter of Amnesty International, heard about the "The Kid's Campaign," he volunteered to help. Ron's class just had one old computer that he had received from writing a grant. Rick provided the campaign with technology and training. With assistance from other Amnesty volunteers, he brought a van filled with computer equipment to Broad Meadows. The Internet was at its beginning stages. Rick helped the students create a website that the students called "A Bullet Can't Kill a Dream." He taught them how to use the Internet to enhance the campaign. (The website can still be found at http://www.mirrorimage.com/iqbal/.)

In addition to the website the students decided to send letters to schools throughout the United States using the Scholastic Network, an educational link that Mr. Adams found for them. By May 19th, they had received donations from 74 schools totaling over $2,000. Jen recalled, "It just started to spread like wildfire. We were on local news stations. ... Then the guy from channel 5 came to my house and to Amanda's and some of the others to do interviews."

Once the donations began to come in the students realized they needed to open a bank account. Anne Marie Zukauskas knew someone at Hibernia Bank in Quincy. She gave the students his name and told them to write a letter. The letter led to a trip to the bank to open an account. Amanda said: "We went on a little field trip to the bank and we learned all about the process of how to open up a fund. It was awesome."

Donations came from all over the country. Students in other communities ran fundraisers. A high school in Ohio raised $150 from a popcorn sale; a 4-H in Illinois held a pizza sale and raised $280, the Little League in Oklahoma sent $120 (Greenhouse, 1996). Jen said:

I remember our lunch room. … We had meetings a lot there. We had this big poster up of a thermometer for the school. First we thought, we are never going to get past five thousand dollars. It's just not going to happen … and then we were at $10,000!!

The students decided to draw upon the traditions of former Broad Meadows activists and write letters to politicians including state Senators John Kerry and Ted Kennedy. Senator Kerry had an office in Quincy. He met with the students there. He also let them use the office. Senator Kennedy sent the students a handwritten letter of support. He contacted the Pakistani ambassador who got in touch with Prime Minister Benazir Bhutto to gain permission for the students to build a school. Senator Kennedy also visited the students at Broad Meadows. Amanda recalled:

> We wrote Ted Kennedy letters and I think he was truly amazed that there was a group of middle school kids who cared about something other than themselves. We met him several times. He would say "I love kids and I have a large family. I think what you guys are doing to protect other kids in the world is amazing." He (Kennedy) had the power and connections to make things happen and he was willing to come forward to help us.

As the campaign grew, an informal "Kid's Campaign" community began to emerge. Approximately 102 students participated. There was a core group of 12–14 students who Jen referred to as the "pinnacle people." These were the students who consistently worked on the campaign all the way through. However, because the structure was informal and welcoming students could participate and contribute in their own ways when they had the time and inclination. Friday meetings were open meetings.

Students began to adopt specific roles that became a source of their identities in the campaign. Amanda took on the role of a spokesperson and activist. She learned to write and deliver a variety of speeches. She gave informational speeches about Child Labor and the Kid's Campaign, recruitment speeches, speeches to solicit donations, and acceptance speeches when the group won awards.

She was active in developing the project and its goals. Jen became the project's business manager. She kept track of all of the records: the donations, speaking engagements, correspondence. She organized everything using a shorthand system that she developed. She did everything manually on big yellow pads. Computers were just coming in at the time and there was one computer in the room. It took close to a half an hour for the students to get online if the modem was working, so Jen opted for pencils and paper. Ron called Jen "The Captain."

The students, with a bit of nudging from Mr. Adams, decided that they would write a personal thank you note for each of the 3,000 donations that they had received. They decided to meet in the mornings before school to write the notes. Mr. Adams and some of the other teachers rotated early mornings to facilitate the students' endeavor. Many of the donations were sent directly to the bank and weekly afternoon field trips to the bank became a regular routine of the campaign. Jen kept track of the donations and notes.

Ron said, "When they read the letters, they were reading encouragement." Amanda recalled,

> We would get donations and sometimes there would be letters with them. My heart would fill with happiness. For me, each donation was someone who believed in what we were doing and in Iqbal's dream. I wanted each person to have their hearts touched by Iqbal like ours were.

Many individuals who received the students' notes were moved by them and contributed again. Jen wrote to a woman from California thanking her for her contribution and received the following promise of future contributions.

> Dear Jennifer,
>
> Thank you for your letter to acknowledge our contribution to your Iqbal Campaign. And for the update on where your work is. I am very moved by the project, both because of Iqbal's story and because of the work you are doing and the experience you are acquiring. When I was in high school, I instigated a similar project and it taught me the valuable lesson that it is very possible to do good in the world, and that good people are always available to further our efforts to help.
>
> My husband and I would like to promise to you a further incentive. When you reach each new five thousand dollar mark (at 30, 35, 40, 45 and 50,000), we will donate an additional one thousand dollars. For a total of five thousand more by the time you reach your new goal of $50,000.
>
> I wish you great success not only in finding the money but in working with Senator Kennedy's Office and the Pakistani government to get the school built.
>
> Keep me posted on your results and write to me directly to receive the additional one thousand dollars at each mark.
>
> Merry Christmas to you and your classmates.

As the school year came to a close students organized summer thank you note sessions because the donations kept coming in. Thank you note writing became a way for students who were not "pinnacle people" to contribute to the campaign. It also became an entry point for newcomers.

STUDENT VOICES: ELLAINE

Ellaine was born in the Philippines. She moved to Seattle at age 2 and then to Quincy at age 6. She is the youngest of four children. Her mom was a teacher in the Philippines and worked as a librarian at the Boston Public Library in the United States. Her father had been a merchant marine and worked for an oil company when he came to Massachusetts.

Ellaine was in the 6th grade when Iqbal visited Broad Meadows. She had heard about his visit and the aftermath, but didn't become involved in the campaign until she entered the 7th grade when she was a student in Mr. Adams' English class. Her journey from newcomer to key activist at the heart of the organization demonstrates the openness and fluidity of The Kid's Campaign Community. She said:

> I think that I just heard about it as an after school program. It was advertised like "Come to this meeting and hear about this campaign" and that's how it started; I came to the first meeting and had a good time. I thought it was interesting, and I think being that young and hearing about all of the injustice that's happening—you get all fired up ...

Ellaine started by writing thank you notes before school. She would arrive at 7:00 about three days a week and would meet with the other students in the cafeteria. They were provided with official stationary; photo copied sheets of paper and a template with basic information. They then received copies of checks or someone's letter and which they would read and then they would write responses and try to clear the pile. She said:

> It was really important to write. People were taking their time to contribute to what we were doing. It was so cool to really thank them. That little interaction was nice. It was important to show our gratitude in that personal way.

As she became more involved she began to go on the after school trips to the bank. Ellaine said:

> I remember going to the bank a lot. ... We would go in and deposit the money and it was a big deal because they had free popcorn. We'd go to the bank, deposit money and see how much was in there and then eat some free popcorn and sometimes Mr. Adams would treat us to Wendy's.

In addition to thank you note writing, Ellaine began to attend the weekly meetings on a regular basis. She gradually moved from novice to active participant. Ellaine remembers the after school meeting as being large, "hefty between 30 to 50 students, although some of them just wrote thank you notes." She started to accompany the "pinnacle people" when they went on speaking engagements and she would observe the other students present.

In November 1995, Reebok announced that The Kid's Campaign was one of the winners of the Youth in Action Award, the same award that Iqbal Masih had won the previous year. Reebok donated $12,000 to the School for Iqbal project. The Awards Ceremony was held in New York at the Apollo Theater in Harlem. Amanda, Jen, and Ellaine were part of the group of 12 students that went to New York to accept the award. Amanda was one of the spokespersons. Both Mr. Adams and Mrs. Zukauskas accompanied them.

At the awards ceremony the students had the opportunity to meet the other award recipients and learn about their struggles for Human Rights. The honorees included Angela Brown, a student/youth organizer from Georgia, who developed an organizational network to fight for environmental injustice in the southeast; Richard Nsangabaganwa of Rwanda who worked as a chief investigator in order to bring justice to the victims of genocide in his country; Miguel de los Santos de Cruz, a Mexican lawyer, who defended indigenous peoples whose human rights had been violated. The fourth honoree, Van. Phantom Nyidron, a Tibetan Buddhist nun, was unable to attend as she was serving a 17-year prison sentence for protesting the Chinese occupation of Tibet ("Reebok Human Rights," 1995). Ellaine said:

> I remember all of the stories. There were little videos of what the winner had accomplished. Everyone's journey and then the person would come on stage to speak and receive the award. With the Tibetan Buddhist Nun, it was really dramatic because they showed the video and then she couldn't come to accept the award because she was in jail. That really made an impression on me.

The students also met actors and sports celebrities who were actively involved in human rights work. These included Richard Gere, Susan Sarandon, Peter Gabriel, Michael Stipe, Gregory Hines, Ziggy Marely, Gregory Thomas, and Venus Williams.

Amanda and Amy, another active spokesperson, accepted the award on behalf of The Kid's Campaign and appealed to the audience to help them raise funds for Iqbal's school. After the ceremony, audience members visited the tables manned by the ten other students. They took flyers, bought t-shirts, and made donations totaling 800 dollars.

Amanda felt that this event was different from the others because of the preparation involved. Prior to the event Reebok representatives came to Broad Meadows with speech writers who did two workshops with Amanda and Amy. The students wrote their own speeches but the speechwriters helped them tweak and shorten the speeches so they fit into an allotted time frame. They also prepped the students on etiquette—how to present yourself at a public forum, how to do a press conference.

Amanda remembers being moved by the other award winners' stories. She also recalls being incredibly nervous, tripping a little going up the stairs to receive the award, and then the speech going incredibly well. After the speech there was a press conference. There was a table with name tags and she was seated next to Richard Gere. She described the experience as "amazing."

Ellaine worked at one of The Kid's Campaign tables, answering questions and accepting donations. She felt that they were successful in raising awareness about child labor and the campaign. She said:

I think that everywhere we went, even if we weren't talking to news people—we were talking to people who were intrigued and interested in what we were doing. At that point, I could talk about it forever.

By the spring, The Kid's Campaign had raised over $100,000 and the students had to decide who they were going to trust with the money. They reached out to Amnesty International, Reebok, and Senator Kennedy's office. Doug Khan from Reebok came to the school and taught the students how to request a proposal. The next step was to contact human rights groups to get a list of organizations that could build a school in Pakistan. They received lists from Amnesty International, UNICEF, and Doctors without Borders. The students then wrote letters to thirty organizations and asked them what they would do with the $100,000. Twelve proposals came back.

Amanda remembered feeling overwhelmed. "We worked so hard to raise the money and it was like how do we know that these people are legitimate. What if they just take the money? We wanted everything to fit Iqbal's dream."

Jen said:

We felt really pressured by the adults. They all wanted the money. We kept getting e-mails pressuring us to go with their organization. ... It was one of our biggest decisions. We didn't want to partner with someone who would tarnish our image and everything we had worked for and get the, "I told you so."

The students conducted research on the nonprofit organizations that applied for the funds. Reebok and Amnesty International did background checks and shared their findings with the students.

Before they cast the final vote, Ron asked if the group could meet at the Church of the Presidents, the Unitarian church where John and Abigail Adams are buried. The curator agreed. Ron had the students separate. Each one sat in silence at a different pew for 15 minutes. Ron said, "They were awesome. They just sat with their eyes closed and thought about an answer." After meditating they argued and debated. Then they voted by secret ballot.

They selected the Pakistani agency SUDHAAR. The agency was located near Muridke, where Iqbal was raised. The students felt that the agency's knowledge of the region would be essential as they would better understand local problems. The agency had already built one school and proposed a transitional program where working children and those at risk for child labor could get an education.

Kasur, a town 57 miles from Muridke, was recommended as the school site. The proposal suggests SUDHAAR would build a nonformal primary education center for children ages four to twelve that would serve 200 children. It would be geared toward two groups, children already working in the three area industries: tanneries, cloth weaving, and *darris* (large floor mats) industry and those at high risk of becoming child laborers.

The school would offer the primary curriculum over a period of 40 months and every eight months the students would move up if they passed an internal assessment. Teachers would be trained to use a teaching methodology different than the standard pedagogy used in traditional Pakistani schools. It would be more learner centered and encourage the students to express themselves through art and creative writing.

The agency also proposed the development of a microcredit program for families with members in bonded labor. The purpose of the program was to provide families credit and training in a craft so that they could free themselves and their children who were in bonded labor and become self-employed.

One of SUDHAAR's major objectives was to make the school self-sustaining after three years. They proposed the establishment of an Iqbal Education Foundation which would be comprised of distinguished individuals and organizations in the fields of basic human rights. The foundation would honor Iqbal's memory and the school's goal of providing education for children in forced labor or at risk of becoming bonded or forced laborers. The five-room school opened in November 1996. The following year the small credit program began. Fifty families were able to buy back their children from bondage.

The school hired more teachers and instituted teacher training so that the program could become self-sufficient. The teachers had the equivalent of an 8th-grade education. When the first class at the school sat for the national literacy exam, 80% of the students in the school passed the exam.

The school was a success. After the third year, the Iqbal Education Foundation took over the daily operating expenses. SUDHAAR has continued to create other schools based on this model. The only part of the original plan that was discontinued was the microcredit program to buy back children from bonded or forced labor. Initially this program had an 80% success rate. However, as time went on there were many scams to get the money and the program had to be discontinued.

Today, upon entering the school one will see the following inscription:

> This school conceived by the school children of Broad Meadows is in memory of Iqbal Masih and is dedicated to all the working children of the world. A bullet cannot kill a dream.

CONCLUSION

As The Kid's Campaign developed it began to exhibit the characteristics of an emergent community of practice. For a learning community to be considered a community of practice there must be a domain or a shared endeavor and a commitment to the endeavor; community, a sense of belonging to a group that engages in activities, discussions and information sharing, and practice, a shared repertoire of resources, experiences, stories, tools, and ways of addressing problems (Wenger, 1998).

Prior to Iqbal's visit, Ron had started to alter the hierarchical student/teacher relationship through the introduction of youth participation and democratic practice in both the classroom and in student-initiated projects that extended beyond the classroom. The structure for student-initiated projects before and after school meetings was also in place and was supported by the administration.

Once The Kid's Campaign began, Ron and the students had to construct and negotiate the roles and boundaries for the youth and adult allies for the community to function in a more egalitarian manner. This dilemma is typical in youth programs that take place in informal settings such as after school programs or in programs based in community organizations (Zeldin, Larson, Camino, & O'Connor, 2005).

Research on youth programs that depend on youth/adult partnerships generally refers to such programs as adult-driven programs where adults have greater control and youth have input or youth-driven programs where the youth have greater control but the adults have input. Since a primary goal of youth civic action programs is to promote youth leadership, they largely fall into the youth-driven camp (Larson, Walker, & Pearce, 2005).

The dilemma facing adult allies in youth-led programs is that youth are new to civic action work and often lack the necessary tools and skills that more experienced adults have to make the project a success. The issue then becomes when should the adult mentors intervene and/or provide assistance and guidance in a program that is geared to promote democracy, participation, and empowerment.

Kirshner (2006) argues that theories of apprenticeship learning offer a way to avoid the "youth-led vs adult-led trap." Kirshner describes an apprenticeship as "participation in a collaborative activity, in which novices receive just enough guidance from experts to pursue a shared goal"(p. 42). In such cases, adults intervene to provide what Kirshner calls modeling, coaching, and fading. They also help students make contacts in the adult world and provide background information when needed. Through the apprenticeship students develop an array of academic and real-world skills.

In their seminal text, *Situated Learning: Legitimate Peripheral Participation (1991)*, Lave and Wenger examine how apprentices learn in communities of practice. They focus upon the ways that novices acquire skills and group identity. They coined the term legitimate peripheral participation to refer to the variety of legitimate, genuine, meaningful experiences (such as thank you note writing) open to newcomers who wish to participate at some level or become more fully involved and move from novice to full participant in the community. In the context of after school activist or service programs full participation often entails taking on leadership roles.

The Kid's Campaign presented the emergent community with a unique set of challenges as no one in the community, including Ron, had prior experience building a school in a foreign country. Mechanisms for fund-raising were non-existent and needed to be developed. They also needed to devise ways to work with existing contacts to develop the networks necessary to build a school in Pakistan. In addition, as the community evolved they needed to negotiate roles and boundaries and create meaningful participatory experiences for students who wanted to participate in a small way as well as pathways for newcomers who wanted to become full participants and take on leadership roles.

The community developed along the lines of the youth-centered apprenticeship model. The democratic structure developed in earlier campaigns was transferred and coconstructed to fit the needs of The Kid's Campaign. The students debated and decided to adhere to the following rules:

Anyone in the school is welcome to participate in the campaign.
They can participate in whatever way they can.
There are no mandatory requirements.
At meetings, anyone can speak, but only one person can speak and at a time.
You can't cut any one off, mock or criticize what anyone says.
All decisions are put to a vote and the majority rules.

Ron took on the role of a facilitator and supported the students' decision to build a school in Iqbal's memory. He also encouraged them to develop and supported their fund-raising ideas. When tasks arose where students needed assistance Ron would assume the role of mentor and model and coach the skills. He did this when it came to speech writing and public speaking, but as Amanda testified, he "kept it real," providing guidance but never superimposing his views or language on the students. Jen said:

> He'd have everyone write down their speeches individually. Then he'd review them to make sure the grammar was correct. I mean who is a better teacher advisor to have than an English teacher. Then he would have the students practice saying the speeches, so that they didn't rush through them or anything.

Ellaine also remembered the training in public speaking. She said:

We would just practice reading the speeches and he would be very diligent and say things like "Pause when you say this" or "People might clap after you say this." We would write that in our notes. Then we would type the speeches really big and in parentheses write "pause" or "take a breath," or "emphasize this word," and I think that was my first real training in public speaking.

Ron also helped them to connect to other adult allies who intermittently provided coaching and/or resources. Rick Roth from Amnesty International donated technology and showed them how to build and operate a website. The principal Anne Marie Zukauskas provided a contact at the local bank who taught the students how to open and manage an account. When the Campaign won the Reebok Youth Award, Reebok sent professionals from its staff to help the students shape their speeches. Ted Kennedy, then Senator from Massachusetts, responded to the students' letters, visited the school, and spoke with Benazir Bhutto and other high-ranking Pakistani officials to gain permission for the school to be built.

Students, with Ron's assistance, again reached out to adult allies once they had finished fund-raising. Reebok provided training on how to request a proposal. Human Rights groups and Senator Kennedy's office provided lists of legitimate NGOs within Pakistan.

Perhaps the most challenging negotiation of roles came when the students had to select an agency to build a school. Both Ron and the students were involved with developing the criteria for analyzing the proposals. Ron encouraged them to research the agencies requesting money and they learned work collaboratively in solving this real-life problem. Jen said:

> I was in eighth grade and we had to have a conversation about what we were going to do and Mr. Adams was fantastic with that. He always left the decisions to us. I can remember sitting in this room. We stayed in there like for two or three hours just hashing over the pros and cons. We had those big sheet boards with long sheets of paper on them and we would rip off the sheets of paper and write these are the pros and cons of this organization and we would tack them on the wall.

Jen and Amanda were founding members of the School for Iqbal. Ellaine's experience demonstrates the types of participatory opportunities that evolved for newcomers who wished to become full participants and take on leadership roles. In 7th grade, she began by attending the Friday meetings. Then she started coming before school to write thank you notes. As she became more involved she joined the trips to the bank and observed the presentations given by the "pinnacle people" at various events. When she entered 8th grade Ellaine became a leader in the program and wrote and delivered speeches on the campaign's behalf.

While Amanda, Jen, and Ellaine agree that adult allies played a critical role in The Kid's campaign, they believe that the program succeeded because it was student initiated and students felt a sense of ownership of the project. Amanda said:

> When I see all these after school groups that are started and don't succeed, it's really sad to me. It's because the students aren't given the opportunity to make the decisions and, make it feel like their own. ... It was our idea and we voted, we were a democracy. We chose what was going on. ... And we had people like Mr. Adams that advocated for kids who have the ideas and want to be heard and want to change the world for better.

Chapter 4

Impact of The Kid's Campaign on the Lives of the Student Activists

Because learning transforms who we are and what we can do, it is an experience of identity. It is not just an accumulation of skills and information, but a process of becoming—to become a certain person or, conversely, to avoid becoming a certain person.

—Etienne Wenger, 1998

When Iqbal spoke with us, he made me look at what I had differently. He showed me that it was wrong to take things for granted. And it is important to speak out against things that are wrong. I thought if Iqbal could make a difference, so could I.

—Amanda, age 14, Boston Globe Interview, 1995

The campaign's success altered the lives of many Pakistani child laborers by providing them with the opportunity to receive a basic education at the new school. It also impacted the lives of the Quincy student activists who participated in The Kid's Campaign and led to gains in characteristics associated with "positive youth development."

In their study of student voice initiatives, Mitra and Serriere (2012) found that participation initiatives enhanced students' sense of agency, civic efficacy, and competence. They define these terms in the following manner: agency or the ability to "act or exert influence and power in a given situation"; civic efficacy, "the belief that one can make a difference in one's social world"; and competence, the development of "new skills and abilities, active problem solving as well as being appreciated for one's talent" (pp. 745–746).

Throughout their interviews, Amanda, Jen, and Ellaine all described experiences and voiced feelings that demonstrated developing senses of agency, civic efficacy, and competence as a result of participation in The Kid's Campaign.

AMANDA: THE MAKING OF AN ACTIVIST

Amanda described her childhood as "really traumatic." As a young girl her best friend in 1st and 2nd grade was diagnosed with a tumor and died. Her parents divorced shortly afterward and she became very withdrawn, and quiet. At varying intervals, she and her brother, two years her junior, lived with their mother at a trailer park in Scappoose or with her father and her stepmother, Lynn, and her daughter, Heather, in Portland. Amanda said:

> My Mom was a working Mom, so my brother and I spent a lot of time healing ourselves and kind of raising ourselves. Because back then, you were left at home at seven, eight years old and you did what you had to do.

At the end of 6th grade, Amanda moved with her father, stepmother, and stepsister to Quincy. Her brother remained with her biological mother in Scappoose. Amanda's father had some college background. She described him as "super smart, a walking manual for everything technical." In Oregon, he worked at a plating company, where he almost ran the company. When he first arrived in Quincy, he worked as a garbage man for a while. Then he worked for another plating company and eventually joined the Coast Guard. He currently works as an engineer at the VA hospital.

Her stepmom Lynn had her daughter Heather at eighteen and never went to college. She worked for John Hancock when they moved back to Massachusetts to help support the family.

Amanda remembers being very nervous about the move to Quincy. She feared that she wouldn't fit in and that Quincy kids had more money or were more sophisticated than she was. She was self-conscious about her clothes and her hair. Her mom took her to Bradley's to buy clothes and she feared that the Quincy kids would all shop at Abercrombie and Fitch or Old Navy and would tease her. She said:

> They (the Quincy students) all had accents. I don't know how many times they asked me if I had travelled in a wagon. They were stuck on the Oregon Trail. Going to a new school, starting 7th grade, not knowing who I was, not knowing if I was going to be comfortable living with my Dad and Stepmom. ... I was really scared.

Despite her initial trepidation, Amanda liked being in a bigger city where there was a lot more to do. Scappoose, according to Amanda, was a small town where life revolved around football and everybody knew everybody else's business. Quincy was less cliquish and the schools were better. She really liked the teachers at Broad Meadows.

Looking back, Amanda feels that both her dad and stepmom were very supportive of her education. They helped with homework and encouraged her to get good grades. She described her stepmother as "adamant that they (Amanda and Heather) had the tools to succeed in school." However, they did not discuss the news at home or encourage any kind of social activism or civic involvement. They were very skeptical about her involvement in The Kid's Campaign. She said:

> They thought I was nuts! (However) Meeting Iqbal gave me an outlet. It helped me to focus on something, so that I could feel better about myself and the situation of how I grew up.

Amanda believes that her empathy for Iqbal was connected to her troubled childhood. However, her relationship with Ron Adams and the democratic structure of the program created the safe space she needed to blossom and grow. She described Mr. Adams as a "second Dad." Due to their economic circumstances, her stepmom and dad had to work all the time, but Ron stayed after school with them and gave them constant encouragement and support.

Amanda always loved school, but after meeting Iqbal, she said that she "embraced it even more." She began to realize that education wasn't a "chore, but a right" that she was lucky to have.

The "pinnacle people" in the campaign were known for their work in the Broad Meadows student community and were often teased and made fun of by other students. They were called "geeks, brown-nosers, and the Iqbal kids." Amanda felt that the students who made fun of them weren't opposed to the work they were doing, but were jealous of the privileges they received. They went on field trips and missed school. If tests were scheduled on their trip days they were allowed to retake them later on. Amanda didn't let the teasing bother her because the campaign gave her an identity. She expressed her growing sense of agency:

> My identity at that point ... in other people's eyes, I was the Iqbal girl. You got made fun of a bit, but in my eyes, I was an activist. I became empowered. I became not afraid if I had an opinion. I just felt better about myself. My self-esteem sky rocketed ... so I guess that it (The Kid's Campaign) became a kind of safe haven for us geeky kids.

The Campaign also boosted Amanda's sense of competency and provided her with numerous real-world skills. She felt that participation in the campaign enhanced her ability to brainstorm ideas, speak publicly, debate ideas, work as part of a team, and to understand financial, marketing, and political strategies. She believed that even her reading comprehension improved through analyzing and evaluating agency proposals to fund the school. She said:

> All of this took place outside the classroom. How crazy is that? It's funny because we have this idea that we have to be in a classroom sitting in a chair, or reading something online, or whatever, to learn about life. But it really happens when you are doing it.

Amanda continued in her role as activist/spokesperson throughout the 8th grade where her sense of civic efficacy continued to blossom. After accepting the Reebok Youth in Action Award with Amy, she and Amy received an invitation from Congressional Representative Joseph P. Kennedy to testify at a forum on child exploitation sponsored by the Congressional Human Rights Caucus on May 23, 1996. The students' role was to bear witness. They shared their knowledge about child labor and what they had learned through their involvement in The Kid's Campaign. Mr. Adams helped them prepare and accompanied them on the trip.

On her return from Washington, DC, Amanda, Ellaine, and several other students spoke about their experience at Harvard Graduate School of Education. Two weeks later The Kid's Campaign was featured on Good Morning America.

Neither her activism nor her relationship with Ron ended upon her graduation from Middle School. Amanda attended the Woodward School for Girls, a private school in Quincy, during her first year in high school. While Amanda, Jen, and other pinnacle people decided it was time to "pass down the torch" and let the students still at Broad Meadows run The Kid's Campaign, Amanda helped out with speaking engagements. On March 26, 1997, Amanda and Ellaine appeared on MTV on a show "Get up, Stand up" that profiled 7 young people from around the world who had received recognition as Human Rights activists.

When 9th grade came to a close, Amanda went back to Oregon to visit her biological mother and she decided to stay. Her mom had another child, a boy, who was born with a serious heart condition. He needed major surgery and Amanda chose to stay and support her mom and stepbrother. In September 1997, Amanda was selected by "Ms. Magazine" as one of twenty women to watch. An article with her picture appeared in the September/October issue.

Amanda was unhappy at Scappoose High School. She felt bored as she had already covered much of school work being presented when she was at Broad Meadows. When Mr. Adams called to see if she would represent The Kid's Campaign on the Global March against Child Labor, she was thrilled.

Through her participation in the Global March her sense of agency, civic efficacy, and competency was further enhanced.

THE GLOBAL MARCH AGAINST CHILD LABOR (GMACL)

The Global March is an international alliance of more than 1,400 organizations in over 100 countries whose goal is to raise awareness of the plight of the 250 million children worldwide who are trapped in the cycle of poverty and child labor. Participants in the 1998 march included activists from NGOs, trade unions, youth organizations, and former child laborers who join in one of four parallel marches in Asia, Africa, Europe, and the Americas.

The marches culminated in Geneva, Switzerland, on June 17, 1998, where a core group of 200 members addressed the International Labor Organization's (ILO) Conference Convention 182 on the worst forms of child labor. The idea for the march was developed by the 2014 Nobel Prize Laureate, Kailash Satyarthi, the founder and chairperson of the South Asian Coalition on Child Servitude. He had used previous marches as means to raise awareness in India.

Each march began with a kick-off event, a demonstration and/or a teach-in at a major urban area. Then a core group would travel by foot, bus, or caravan (mini-van) across the region participating in local events geared to raise awareness and promote advocacy at the national level through pressuring the governments to ratify and enforce existing conventions and laws on child labor and education and promote actions to eliminate the most hazards forms of child labor worldwide through political advocacy and consumer awareness.

The Americas March began in Sao Paulo, Brazil, and arrived in the United States on May 1st. The US march began in Los Angeles and ended in Washington, DC on May 27th. The US march was sponsored by the Robert F. Kennedy Memorial Center for Human Rights and the International Labor Rights Fund. The purpose of the US march was to focus on domestic child labor problems, especially the 230,000 migrant children employed in agriculture and the 13,000 employed in sweatshops. US organizers also focused upon consumer education and hoped to inspire consumers to advocate for child labor-free goods.

Amanda made arrangements to complete her schoolwork and joined the Global March in Los Angeles on May 1, 1998. The march began with a Teach-in on Child Labor. Representatives of the International Labor Organization, local unions, teachers, youth activists, and former child laborers participated in the Teach-in. On May 2nd, there was a rally in Santa Monica followed by a ska concert, "Ska for Children's Rights" at a club in West Hollywood, the Whisky a Go-Go.

The group then traveled by caravan and stopped in San Diego; Tijuana, Mexico; Mexicali, Mexico; Yuma and Tucson, Arizona; El Paso, Texas; Sonora, Mexico; Edinburg, Texas; San Antonio, Texas; Dallas, Texas; Hope, Arkansas; Little Rock, Arkansas; Memphis, Tennessee; St Louis, Missouri; Chicago, Illinois; Detroit, Michigan; Cleveland, Ohio; Pittsburgh, Pennsylvania; New York, New York; Philadelphia, Pennsylvania; and Washington, DC. After spending two days in Washington, the group left for Geneva, Switzerland, on May 28th.

Amanda described the Global March as "Cool, the most amazing thing." While she enjoyed participating in the teach-ins and other events, she felt that she also learned a great deal from interacting with individuals from so many diverse backgrounds. They traveled in mini-van caravans and picked up participants from different countries where the marches were going on simultaneously. Many people from Latin America and Southern Africa joined them. They slept in churches and synagogues across the country. She said:

> I was only allowed to have one duffel bag of clothes and a sleeping bag and a pillow. We would stop in different cities and speak about the hardships that were going on with children all over the world and call upon people to do something.
>
> Once we were supposed to sleep in this church outside of Edinburg, Texas and when we pulled in and the guy saw all of these people of color, he said: "I will not be responsible for anything that happens to you." Literally, 1998 that was said to us. So we decided to spring for a hotel that night because we did not feel safe.

While Amanda was traveling across the United States student activists at Broad Meadows Middle School, in conjunction with the Robert F. Kennedy Memorial Center for Human Rights, devised the Virtual March against Child Labor for youth who wished to support the Global March but could not participate themselves. The goal of the Virtual March was twofold: motivate 3,000 youth to post e-mail messages calling for an end to child labor and present copies of these messages to policy makers attending the ILO Convention in Geneva. Each message posted symbolized a mile and 3,000 messages represented a march across the United States.

Three 8th-grade students from Broad Meadows Middle School accompanied by Ann Marie Zukauskas and Ron Adams met Amanda in Washington, DC to walk in the final segment of the Global March. The Broad Meadows students brought a six-inch black binder that contained e-mail messages of support from youth around the world. They presented the binder to US Labor Secretary Alexis Herman who brought them to the ILO Conference in Geneva.

The United Garment Workers Union sponsored Amanda's trip to Geneva to the ILO Convention. She attended numerous workshops and met Canadian youth activist Craig Kielburger, founder of Free the Children, an NGO designed for youth to help youth around the world.

When Amanda returned from Switzerland she decided to remain in Massachusetts. She finished high school at Quincy High. She began college at the Massachusetts College of Liberal Arts where she started a local activist campaign called Extraordinary Leaders Volunteering in Service or ELVIS. The group raised money for food banks and other local charities. They ran penny drives and on Valentine's Day, a volunteer would impersonate Elvis and deliver songs and candy for a charitable donation.

Amanda transferred to Portland State where she finished her degree in Speech Communications. She feels that her role as speaker activist in The Kid's Campaign influenced her choice of major. It also influenced her elective choices. She took courses in political science, media literacy, and cultural anthropology. She loved learning about other cultures and attributed this interest to her experiences in The Kid's Campaign and the Global March.

The Campaign also influenced her view of citizenship and she feels that in these times we need to be global in our outlook and learn how we can "enhance the livelihoods of all people." She describes herself as an "aware consumer" who still checks labels and tries to buy products that are made without child labor.

Amanda currently lives in Forsythe, Montana, with her husband Dan and two young daughters, Emma and Gwen. Dan works as a conductor on the Burlington Northern Railroad. Amanda still considers herself an activist and is thinking of becoming a teacher and starting democratic activist programs with her future students.

JEN: THE MAKING OF A MANAGER

Jen is Quincy born and bred. Although she moved around a lot as a child, her family always remained within the Quincy City limits. As an adult, Jen has moved around a bit as well, but she has always come back to Quincy.

Like Amanda, Jen was a good student who liked school. In 6th grade she won a scholarship to Milton Academy, a special Saturday enrichment program. Her parents encouraged Jen to do well in school. Her mother modeled the importance of education. She worked as a nursing assistant in a nursing home in Dorchester. She always wanted to be a nurse and would pick up courses whenever she could afford them. She became an LPN when Jen was in middle school and an RN when Jen was in high school.

As a 7th grader, Jen took on the role as manager of the campaign. She was unsure why she selected this role and felt her choice could have been influenced in part by her father, a mailroom operator. She described him as "a constant organizer, very neat and tidy" who oversees the programming of the machines that sort the mail.

Jen's decision to organize and run things contributed to her developing sense of agency, competency, and civic efficacy. She said:

> I was the background person. I coordinated all the paperwork and the mail and the bank ... just making sure it all ran efficiently. If we got mail in, I was the one that recorded everything and opened it. I processed the thank you notes to go back out and made sure that we were always on top of it.
>
> I wasn't a huge public speaker. I did it, but I preferred to leave it to Amanda or Amy. I'd help them write their speeches and make sure that all of the details were in. For me, I didn't need the recognition, I'm not saying that they needed it either, but for me I knew what we were doing was right and I knew that I was doing the work that I was supposed to do.

While Jen's parents approved of her work in the campaign, they hadn't discussed politics or promoted activism or civic work at home. Jen described their response to her involvement in The Kid's Campaign:

> It's weird for my Mom and Dad to this day. They think I'm an alien child because I've always been ... like they never pressured or tried to get me involved in anything. It was always me pushing myself to do different roles. I was always a straight A student. I never got in to trouble, never did anything crazy and I was always involved in different things in school.

Jen intermittently helped out with the campaign after she left Broad Meadows for Quincy High School. She traveled to Minnesota with Amanda and two other girls to accept the Minnesota Advocates for Human Rights Award in 1997 during her sophomore year in high school.

As result of her participation in The Kid's Campaign Jen decided to major in Political Science in college. She attended St. Regis College in Weston, Massachusetts. In addition to the political science major, she minored in Economics and Business. She attributed her choice of minors to the satisfaction she received in her role as manager in the campaign. She spent a semester in London studying economics and traveled in Europe.

Upon graduation, Jen took a customer service job at Unishippers, a Boston area shipping company. She received a series of promotions and became their regional office manager, running the offices in Massachusetts, New York, and Connecticut. Then she was moved up to doing their accounts payable. While working, she obtained two masters degrees online from the University of Phoenix: an MBA and a Masters in Accounting.

Jen is the mother of Isabelle Rose who was two in 2012. At that time, she had accepted a position as Director of Finance at G-Forth Shipping and was looking to buy a house in Quincy with her boyfriend, a truck driver who is Isabelle's dad.

Jen believes that the Human Rights Curriculum and Kid's Campaign affected the environment of Broad Meadows and had a strong impact on her worldview at a critical time in her life. She felt that the discussions the students had in Mr. Adams and Ms. Willoughby's classes made the school a "more welcoming community" and because of this "a lot of kids tried to come to school without judgments of kids from different backgrounds." She feels this openness was most evident in The Kid's Campaign. She said, "There were people from all backgrounds and no one cared. We welcomed anyone who wanted to help. We were very open with it."

As an adult she feels that her participation in the campaign has affected her views of citizenship and believes that good citizens need to take responsibility at local, national, and global levels. This attitude manifests itself most prominently in her behavior as a consumer. She constantly looks at labels and tries to buy items that are "marked fair trade." When a relative gave her daughter a gift of Nike sneakers, she returned them and she would never buy a rug that does not have the Goodweave label.

Jen's participation in The Kid's Campaign, especially the sense of competence that she developed in her role as manager, helped to shape her. She said:

> The Kid's Campaign affected who I became. It really pushed me. I didn't like to speak in public, but I loved math. I took on the management role and it guided me throughout my life. I loved being able to turn around to Mr. Adams and tell him exactly what had been accomplished and exactly what needed to be done. I felt really competent with numbers, setting goals and organizing end goals. It is what I thrived at the most.

ELLAINE: A PUBLICIST IN THE MAKING

Ellaine is the youngest of four children. Her eldest sister is fifteen years her senior. Her second sister is 13 years older and her brother, although closest in age, is 8 years older than Ellaine. The family left the Philippines when Ellaine was 2. When she was four she was sent back and lived with her aunts for a year. Her family moved from Dorchester to Quincy when she was five. While Ellaine's childhood and youth was spent in the United States, she believes that part of the reason she was drawn to The Kid's Campaign was her knowledge of poverty in the Philippines. She said:

> Because the Philippines is a third world country, I did have an image of what poor people were like, and hearing about the poverty in another country and little kids being abused was tough. ... I think that I could visualize it more

because I had seen poverty on another level: squatters and kids with no shoes
... but after seeing poverty in the Philippines I knew what poverty was like and
how serious it can get. I think that was an influence.

In Ellaine's family, the emphasis upon education was very strong. Her
mother, a teacher in the Philippines and librarian in the United States, and
dad, a former merchant marine who worked for an oil company, made sure
their children's studies came first. All four of their children attended college.
While her parents did not discuss current events or emphasize social activism,
they were very proud of her work on The Kid's Campaign. She said:

My parents were supportive and they were happy I was doing something con-
structive. I don't think they really understood the impact (of the campaign) until
we were going to New York to accept a giant award and we would go to places
like Harvard University, and give a talk to people twice our age about what we
were doing. I would bring home a clip of us on the news; and then they were
kind of in awe. They were happy and they still love to talk about it and tell
people what we did.

Although Ellaine was a student in Mr. Adams' 7th-grade English class and
participated in the Human Rights curriculum, she was surprised and touched
to learn that Mr. Adams had started the program to minimize the prejudice
Asian immigrants would experience upon entering Broad Meadows. She
said that she never personally experienced prejudice at the school, but "it
depended upon who you talked to ... different people had different experiences." However, she never heard of anyone experiencing prejudice at The
Kid's Campaign. She said, "The environment was really welcoming. What
you were willing to contribute was what mattered."

Ellaine's sense of agency, civic efficacy, and competence increased as a
result of her participation in The Kid's Campaign. She felt that she learned
how to speak in public, at diverse venues that included addressing peers,
speaking at Harvard, and appearing in a film produced by the American
Federation of Teachers. She said:

It definitely helped my confidence, with speaking and learning how to present
myself. ... I learned to how to work together (with peers) and make decisions
as a group ... how to be diplomatic and play nice. It taught me how to meet a
goal. I learned how to be organized and how to manage time. At that point in
my life, I was doing a lot but I was also doing my best to get the best grades
I could at school.

When she entered 9th grade at Quincy High School, Ellaine continued to
work with the campaign. She then moved into other activities and became

involved in Habitat for Humanity, Student Council, and the Drama Club. However, her participation and role in the campaign served as the primary influence for her choice of public relations major at Hofstra University and subsequent career as a publicist and events planner. Ironically, the sense of fulfillment she received from her role in the campaign is the cause of her current dissatisfaction with her career choice.

Ellaine feels that the reason she loved speaking and doing public relations for The Kid's Campaign was that she passionately believed in what she was promoting. Upon graduation, she found that her options in the public relations industry did not lead to that kind of fulfillment. She said:

> I was in the tourism and hospitality industry, and that's just a lot of developers and people with money that want you to get people to pay way too much money for a hotel room. So I wasn't really passionate about it, and especially when in New York; that industry takes a lot of time, and I was working a lot of hours and I was travelling a lot, and it's not what I want to do.
>
> I want to have a life, and spend time with my husband and family and have a family of my own. So that is where I am right now; I'm trying to find something that I can have a bit more of a work/ life balance with something I can really stand behind. It doesn't have to be saving the world, it just has to be something I can stand behind.

Ellaine currently lives in the Windsor Terrace section of Brooklyn with her husband Jeff, who works in the IT sector. They recently had a daughter, Sophie Grace. Ellaine's main focus is on family. She has two part-time jobs. She works from home for an NGO, Arctic Circle. The organization's primary focus is on how the Arctic Circle develops. She does research and marketing and has worked with the president of Iceland. She also does events planning for a company, Bamboo London.

The campaign influenced her view of citizenship and at times she has seen herself as a local, national, or global citizen. She explained:

> My view that it is situational and changes with my life circumstances. Right now my emphasis is on the local because I just had a baby. My twelve year old self, my ideal self, would probably say I am a global citizen. My emphasis will probably change as my life changes and I have more time.

Ellaine believes that the most long-lasting impact of her youthful activism has been on her behavior as a consumer, her awareness, and her career choice:

> At times it affects my behavior as a consumer, but not as much as I would like because I don't have enough money to be pure. However, I would never buy a hand-made rug that wasn't Goodweave. I try to buy Fair Trade food items.

I was in a food coop that made these things affordable. I wouldn't be an aware consumer or be as aware of humanitarian issues, if I hadn't participated in The Kid's Campaign.

It also affected my career choice. I developed confidence as a spokesperson and enjoyed doing publicity for the Campaign. I was able to build upon skills that had become a strength for me. The most important thing I learned from the campaign was that I could make a difference.

CONCLUSION

Amanda, Jen, and Ellaine's self-reflective interviews reveal several common themes. Prior to becoming activists in the campaign, all three young women described themselves as good students who liked school, yet they felt that they didn't totally fit into the "dominant" school culture.

As indicated, in the previous chapters, activism was part of the school culture and students such as Amanda, Jen, and Ellaine knew about the successful campaigns that previous students had developed and carried out. Not only was the structure in place, but the students had positive role models, who might not have mirrored the dominant middle school culture, but were rewarded and respected nonetheless. Amanda fondly refers to the campaign as a "safe haven for geeks" and Ellaine describes it as a place where "prejudice didn't exist and you were valued for what you contributed."

Wenger (1998) states that for education to be transformative, it must open up identities and help individuals explore new ways of being (p. 263). He believes that identity development is a fluid and ongoing process that occurs as individuals participate in multiple communities of practice throughout their lives. When individuals begin to participate in a community they learn to master its practices and develop its beliefs, attitudes, and values.

Whether the community is a sports team, a school chorus, religious youth group, a math class, or an activist campaign, individuals develop their identities and sense of competence if they choose (and have access to) full participation. Conversely, limited participation or nonparticipation can also become a source of identity. Communities can be active spaces where individuals are currently involved or they can be latent and exist "among people who share past histories and can use these histories as resources" (p. 228).

According to Wenger, an individual's identification and sense of belonging to a given community is enhanced by three overlapping modes of belonging: engagement, imagination, and alignment .Engagement refers to the individual's direct experiences in the practices of the community. Imagination refers to the ability to step out of their immediate environment and see the way their learning and activities fit in the world and in their lives beyond the immediate community. Alignment is the manner through which they come to see themselves as a part of something bigger than themselves (pp. 174–180).

All three young women felt that their participation in The Kid's Campaign was a transformative life experience. By mastering the skills and values they associated with becoming "pinnacle people" in the campaign they developed a sense of competence and confidence. They were exposed to and had the opportunity to try out a variety of adult roles: business manager, publicist, activist and imagine themselves using these skills and fulfilling these roles as adults. Participation enhanced their sense of belonging and they came to see themselves as a part of something larger than themselves, activists in the struggle to end child labor, global citizens, and individuals with social consciences who can change the world.

The campaign's most striking impact is the influence their campaign roles had on their choices of college majors and careers. All three women directly link the sense of competence and agency they experienced in the roles they took on in the campaign to these choices. Their roles in the campaign were the only "adult-like" roles they experienced in their schooling prior to entering college.

Amanda, Jen, and Ellaine indicated that they would still like to participate in work that had the potential to make the world a better place. They felt that their sense of purpose made the roles they took on in the campaign personally meaningful. However, while Amanda, Jen, and Ellaine were able to further develop their communications, managerial and public relations skills at the university level, they felt that they lacked access to the types of positions that would allow them to use these skills to promote social change. As a consequence they have modified their goals. Amanda hopes to work for change in her local community and work to empower kids as a teacher. Jen wants to use her managerial skills to enhance her work environment and help people in that way. Ellaine's goal is to do publicity and public relations in the nonprofit sector.

They remain globally aware and participation in the campaign continues to influence their behavior as consumers. Again, all three women said they check labels, attempt to buy fair trade products when feasible, and would never buy a rug that did not have a Goodweave label. They attribute this behavior to their participation in The Kid's Campaign over 15 years ago.

Part II

OPERATION DAY'S WORK

Chapter 5

From Norway to the USA

The World is Sick—You are the Medicine.

—ODW, Norway Slogan (Operasjon Dagsverk, n.d.)

ODW, Operasjon Dagsverk, Norway's largest solidarity campaign for youth, marked its 50th anniversary in 2014. The national program began in 1964, at the annual meeting of the School Student Union of Norway. A student activist challenged his peers to improve the world beyond Norway and do something to help youth in poor countries who did not have the same educational opportunities as Norwegian youth. The students decided to convince the school authorities to give them a day off from school each year so they could work to raise money for student-selected programs that would provide educational opportunities for youth in the developing world.

The Norwegian students were inspired by their counterparts in Sweden who had invented the idea to honor Dag Hammarskjold, the 2nd Secretary General of the United Nations. Hammarskjold was killed in a plane crash in 1961. The program which started in Sweden in 1962 was originally called A Day for Dag.

Norway is a country of just four million, yet during its first year approximately 35,000 Norwegian students participated in ODW. They either worked in traditional work settings such as factories and offices, donating their pay, or raised funds informally by selling baked goods, or washing cars or windows. In total, they raised $15,000, which was a significant sum in 1964. The money was used to support educational programs in Algeria (Operasjon Dagsverk, (2015) n.d.).

Today, in addition to Norway and Sweden, ODW programs operate in Denmark, Finland, Germany, Italy, Belgium, and the United States. The Norwegian program has evolved into a national program with a complex organizational structure. More than 120,000 students from schools all over the country volunteer annually. Over the years these student activists have raised more than a billion dollars for youth education programs in 62 countries in Asia, Africa, and Latin America (Operasjon Dagsverk, n.d).

Philosophy

Every year, student volunteers of participating ODW schools are given the last Thursday of October off to work. This workday is preceded by International Week, a 10-day educational program geared to educate the Norwegian students about the project, the project's host country, its people, and their culture. Students also learn about the inequality that causes poverty in the global South. This educational program is central to ODW's mission and philosophy which focuses upon the principles of solidarity, volunteerism, education, and youth.

ODW is a solidarity program, not a charity program. Its purpose is to foster respect between youth living in the global North and global South. The organization does not want Norwegian students to volunteer out of a sense of pity or guilt. It aims to develop empathy, righteous indignation, and respect—solidarity. To meet this goal during International Week students are exposed to host country's strengths. They learn about the host country's art, literature, music, and history. Ten guest speakers from the project country come to Norway and visit the schools (Operasjon Dagsverk, n.d.; Brustad, 2014).

The importance of Solidarity is described on the *Operasjon Dagsverk* website:

> The solidarity principle is one of the most crucial aspects of Operation Day's Work. For ODW, solidarity is about our shared responsibility for equal opportunity. ... ODW wishes to contribute to a more diversified picture of the South and to question the sometimes simplistic and occasionally damaging presentation of the situation in Africa, Asia and South America in the Norwegian public domain. We aim at emphasizing Equality. (2008, para 4)

When International Week comes to a close it is up to the students to decide if they wish to volunteer to do a day's work to support the project. Volunteerism, like solidarity, is a key principle of ODW.

Education and youth are also central to the ODW philosophy. Therefore, to qualify for ODW support, projects must provide sustainable education and training programs for youth in Africa, Asia, or Latin America. In keeping with the solidarity principle, projects are administered by local organizations in the host country who understand the issues best. The notion that ODW is developed by, for, and with youth is also a vital element of ODW's worldview and mission.

Organizational Structure

A volunteer organization of this magnitude needs a sophisticated organizational structure. Between five and six thousand students organize the ODW campaign each year at the national, district, and school levels. Student participation and democratic practice are key components of both the organization and the campaign.

Each year, an ODW Governing Board is elected by the Norwegian School Student Union, a national student organization that is comprised of 500 students from all over the country. The Governing Board oversees the economic, legal, and organizational aspects of the ODW campaign. The Governing Board, in turn, appoints the National Committee and lays down the financial guidelines for the project.

The National Committee is based in Oslo and consists of 9 to 11 members including the ODW President. This Committee coordinates the daily operations of the campaign at the national level. They produce all of the informational materials and help the District Committees with their work. The Committee publishes a magazine about the project and the culture and history of the host country that is distributed to students in all participating schools. They also produce a Teacher's Guide, stickers, slide shows, and radio and TV spots for district and school distribution. National Committee members exemplify the spirit of volunteerism. They work full-time from July until December and do not receive any pay for their work.

Each of Norway's 22 districts has a committee that includes a chair and between 5 and 12 members. They coordinate International Week within the District. They recruit schools and arrange three seminars about the project for the members of the school committees. They also organize seminars for the teachers. After the campaign has finished the District Committee puts together a final meeting where the program and the campaign are assessed.

Each District Committee has its own website. The following posting from the Østfold District illustrates the spirit of ODW Norway.

Østfold

> Now approaching ODW-autumn fast approaching!
>
> For ODW at your school to be the best possible, we invite you to the district committee for ODW Østfold at your school committee seminar September 19 to 21.
>
> Here you will learn more about ODW, this year's project, North / South issues and useful tips and tricks to arrange ODW. You will also have the opportunity to become familiar with active young people from across the county, and there will of course be much time for social activities and having a blast! (Operasjon Dagsverk, Østfold n.d. 2015)

Each school may enter six participants, but if the school wants to send more, they may apply to dk on ostfold@od.no. We hope the school uses the opportunity to send as many as possible, and preferably more than 6. The more we are together, the happier we are! The school pays 200 kr per participant. You will cover travel and get served everything you need of food and drink at the seminar for free.

We hope to see YOU at the seminar and sjukt gira! (Operasjon Dagsverk, Østfold, n.d.)

The school representatives who attend the district events form the school committees. The district committees organize three seminars in the fall to educate the school committees on the year's project. They also arrange a training seminar for participating teachers. The students on the school committee organize International Week and the workday at their school. After the ODW campaign has been completed, the district committees organize an additional seminar to assess the program and the campaign.

At the middle and high schools, teachers assist in providing instruction during International Week. In addition to attending training seminars, teachers have access to a teaching portal that includes articles and lesson ideas for several subject areas. These include student-centered lessons that use techniques such as simulation and role play. All of the curriculum materials are aligned with the Norwegian curriculum competence goals and focus on the importance of international knowledge and global understanding.

In addition to the various committees, a Project Council composed of 6 adults with extensive experience in foreign aid and the student leaders from the past four ODW campaigns serve ODW in an advisory capacity. Each year Norwegian nongovernmental organizations (NGOs) submit proposals to ODW. These Norwegian Aid Organizations work with partner organizations in the host countries that run the day-to-day project operations. Project Council members review the proposals and select three projects that best meet ODW criteria.

Schools that have participated in ODW over the past two years receive information about project finalists. The school committee runs a democratic election where the entire student body can vote for the project they wish to fund. Each school then sends a representative to the National Student Union's General Assembly Meeting. Representatives of the Norwegian NGOs present their proposed projects. After the presentations, student council delegates and school representatives discuss and debate the proposals' merits and vote to select the project.

ODW raises approximately 3 million dollars in aid annually. Finances are managed by the ODW Secretariat which is composed of three paid full-time adult employees. The Secretariat also monitors ongoing ODW projects.

One Secretariat member serves as secretary to the Project Council. These are the only paid employees in the entire organization.

In 2014, ODW funded programs that provided opportunities for the education of girls in Malawi and Ethiopia. Past projects include funding for programs that provide education and alternative activities for youth living in poverty in Brazilian ghettos; education for youth with disabilities in Malawi, Mozambique, South Africa, and Uganda; literacy education and small business loans for unmarried girls between the ages of 11 and 19 living in rural Bangladesh; and vocational training for youth in Honduras, Nicaragua, and Guatemala (Brustad, 2014).

ODW USA

USAID Pilot Program

ODW Norway caught the attention of Brian Atwood, Bill Clinton's Administrator of the United States Agency for International Development (USAID). He sought to emulate this model and bring ODW to the United States in the 1990s. Atwood and his staff believed that a program like ODW would open the eyes of American youth and help them to understand the necessity of foreign aid programs now and in the future. He needed American models, youth global aid action projects that had succeeded. When he learned about The Kid's Campaign to Build a School for Iqbal, he contacted Ron Adams and asked if he could speak with the Broad Meadows students to find out what they had learned from their experiences.

Ron remembers the day of Brian Atwood's visit:

> He showed up to the school all by himself … took a taxi from Logan Airport and walked into the school. Quite honestly, most of us did not realize the power that he had. He just looked like an average citizen coming to a parent teacher conference. He met with probably two dozen of our School for Iqbal leaders in the Broad Meadows media center. He just sat with them and asked "What did you do?"… "What did you learn?" …
>
> After listening to the students' passionate responses, he asked, "Are you going to retire now, after everything that you have learned or are you interested in continuing this kind of work in more places that just Pakistan?"

Atwood explained the mission and practice of ODW Norway and invited Broad Meadows Middle School to become a pilot school for the program in the United States. Ron said:

> I agreed at the time that we don't create enough opportunities for kids to have these types of experiences. This would be a structured one, encouraged by

USAID, and that would give legitimacy to this pilot project. The kids were excited that their work had been recognized, so we said yes.

Seven other schools across the United States agreed to participate in the pilot program. They included Shorewood Intermediate School in Milwaukee, Wisconsin; Schroeder Middle School in Grand Forks, North Dakota; McFarland Middle School in Washington, DC; Olson Middle School in Minneapolis, Minnesota; Thetford Academy in Thetford, Vermont; Pius IX High School in Milwaukee, Wisconsin; and St. Louis Park Senior High School in St. Louis Park, Minnesota.

At Broad Meadows the framework was already in place. ODW used the same basic structure that had been established during The Kid's Campaign to Build a School for Iqbal. They met every Friday and additional days before or after school when needed. In the beginning the two programs over-lapped as did the leadership. Beth Bloomer, a key ODW leader, began the program in 1997, the last year of the "official" School for Iqbal Campaign, and worked on the online Global March against Child Labor. Beth is one of 7 children, all of whom would become ODW activists at Broad Meadows. She remembered:

> In the beginning, Iqbal's story was the real catalyst for speaking engagements. We took the opportunity to talk about the new effort, Operation Day's Work. We explained its goals and distributed pamphlets to get more schools involved.

Mike, a popular school athlete, joined the following year when he was in 8th grade and soon became an ODW leader. Beth's younger sister Mary followed her lead and joined in 1998. She was in 6th grade. Mike found piloting a new youth organization exciting. He said:

> I didn't really realize what I was getting myself into until I started attending the meetings every Friday. Then I realized how important it was and I just fell in love with the program. The fact that I was involved in starting ODW at Broad Meadows. We were the first group to do it. It was incredible all of the opportunities that we had.

Year 1—Haiti

The first project the students decided to fund during the 1998–1999 school year was the Livestock Training Project for Youth in Haiti, which was admin-istered by a partnership between World Concern Development Project and CARE in Haiti. From their research, the students learned that Haiti was the poorest country in the Western hemisphere and its fragile economy had just been weakened further by a devastating hurricane, Hurricane George.

The project, which the students dubbed "The Goat Project," offered training in livestock care to youth in the poorest regions of Haiti. The project also provided seeds, writing and reading tutors, and instruction in modern farming. Once the training was complete the participants each received a goat. The goat's firstborn was returned to the project to keep the program going.

Prior to the project's start, Beth and two other Broad Meadows students went to Washington, DC to meet with Quincy Congressional delegate, Representative William Delahunt, and representatives from USAID. The students described the methods they had used to develop The Kid's Campaign to build the school in Pakistan. They also shared their goals for child labor and the new project in Haiti. Congressman Delahunt arranged meetings for the students with officials who dealt with child labor issues and had served the state department in Haiti. The students learned about the history, culture, and political environment in Haiti.

Once the school year began, the delegates shared this information with their colleagues in ODW. The group gained additional insights by corresponding with Jeann Robicheau, a Peace Corps volunteer working in Haiti. In her letters, Robicheau described Haitian family life and culture as well as the problems caused by Hurricane George. The students also learned about Haiti from Nanette Caniff, a representative of the St. Boniface Haiti Foundation who had started an orphanage there. She came to ODW meetings and spoke about Haiti.

In November 1998, The Kid's Campaign to Build a School for Iqbal was awarded the USAID Domestic Partnership Award. They were corecipients with Senator Paul Sarbones of Maryland. Ron accompanied three ODW representatives to Washington to accept the award. Ron recalled:

> The presentation was in a huge auditorium with a huge stage and a massive oak podium. ... When the three girls went behind the podium to accept the award all you could see was the top of their heads ... but the kids did a good job. They gave a presentation and there were probably 500 people from USAID attending the ceremony.
>
> For me, witnessing the three girls standing with the US Senator, each with the same award, I thought "Yeah, Brian Atwood is on to something."

The ODW USA Constitutional Convention

ODW USA's first year was a success. Approximately 1,000 students in the US pilot schools participated in the program. They raised over $30,000 for Haitian youth. The next step was to create a structure that was democratic, student centered, and fit the needs of the US constituency. Brian Atwood decided to organize a Constitutional Convention in the Philadelphia area that ran from July 18 to July 23, 1999. One hundred and fifty students and teachers from the pilot schools attended. In addition, there were representatives from schools with an interest in joining the program. Broad Meadows sent Mr. Adams and 22 student representatives including student leaders Beth, Mary, and Michael.

Representatives from USAID, ODW Norway, other youth philanthropy organizations, and prospective funding organizations were also present. A member of the Michigan Community Foundations Youth Programs (MCFYP), Jennifer Zeisler, kept a detailed log of the proceedings which can be found on the web at the Solar Quest School House Report (1999). Student delegates also posted comments on the same site. Jen's log, delegate commentary, along with interview data from Ron, Beth, Mary, and Mike illuminate the week's events.

Jen began her work with the MCFYP at the age of 14. MFYP's goal is to introduce youth to philanthropy at the local level within the state of Michigan. At the time of the ODW Constitutional Convention, Jen was 21. She was selected to represent MCFYP because of her experience, youth, and experience working with youth.

The Constitutional Convention was held at the George School, a Quaker School 27 miles north of Philadelphia. Jen along with the other adult facilitators arrived on July 17th, the day before the convention was scheduled to begin. They met and discussed the convention's design, agenda, and issues facing youth and society. Their dream was that ODW would become a completely student-run organization with programs in every state in the nation in 2003.

According to Jen, buses filled with student delegates and their teachers started arriving at the George School beginning at noon on Sunday, July 17th. The last bus from Grand Forks, North Dakota, ended its 24-hour trek at 5:00. After dinner everyone met at the school meeting house where they were introduced to the facilitators, staff, and guests. Then the students participated in a "personal scavenger hunt," an icebreaker activity where each person was given a list of ten things they needed to find out about other people in the room.

Then Christian Domon from the Haitian project shared the results of students' work during the pilot year. He thanked them on behalf of the Haitian youth who had benefited from the program. Delegate Sasha R wrote a post about his speech on the website:

> Mr. Domon's speech was at first hard to understand. He had an accent. ... I started to use my imagination and began to see the full picture of what he was trying to say. He was amazing. The thoughts he was portraying to us were strong and shocking. I had no idea that an animal could be used as a savings account.

The pictures he used as a help for his presentation were astounding tools. During the presentation I got motivated to work. His words affected me greatly. My spirit for helping people was renewed. All those times that I was working for a charity in school or gave money to a group against poverty, I wasn't sure anymore why and how I was helping. Mr. Domon's presentation reminded me. For the first time I knew how to write the constitution. I knew why I was there (1999).

Beth remembers being really excited about the trip. She had never been to Philadelphia before and felt that it was the perfect choice to write the ODW Constitution. The Broad Meadows delegation thought it was cool to create a constitution in the place the actual constitution was written. They were excited about meeting students from all over the country. However, Beth recalls feeling overwhelmed once they arrived and saw that there were so many students and teachers. Ron Domon's presentation on the Haiti project helped to ground her. Her sentiments were similar to those expressed by Sasha R in her journal. She said:

It was nice to hear firsthand how much the program meant to him and to others in Haiti. It inspired and reinvigorated us and made us want to write a constitution and pick a meaningful project for the next year.

After Mr. Doman's speech the students met with the other students on their halls. Beth said that staying in a dorm was really exciting and fun. There were big rooms with multiple bunks. The girls were in one dorm area; the boys in another. Beth felt that the dorm experience allowed them to bond with other students they knew from ODW in a different and deeper way.

There were also students from other parts of the country. The Broad Meadows group shared the dorm with a group from North Dakota. Beth said, "They thought we had accents and we thought that they had accents. It was kind of fun." At first they spoke about differences between the two states. As the week wore on they would stay up after the sessions and have meaningful discussion on global issues that concerned them. However, on the first night the facilitators asked to discuss their hopes and concerns for the week ahead.

In her journal Jen described Monday, July 19th as an "intense day." The school groups were split up into mixed groups that were called family groups to discuss ideas. They were provided with guide questions that were used to help them develop a Mission Statement. Each family group decided upon a delegate who would share their ideas as a member of the mission statement committee.

The meeting was followed by a presentation by Elvind Dahl of ODW Norway. She shared stories about Norwegian culture and the ODW Norway program. She showed a movie created by Norwegian students, many of whom were present at the constitutional convention.

Lunch followed and more meetings. Students returned to their school groups. They discussed their pilot year and were asked to identify what worked and what needed to change. The school groups shared ideas and artifacts, photographs, and documents that they had created over the course of the year. These were collected to create an ODW toolkit.

The day finished with a group process exercise. The students were divided into mixed school groups and presented with a scenario, a survivor game with a life and death situation. Each group was given the tools that would allow them to survive. They needed to use the tools to determine a way out of the situation. They needed to listen to each other really think outside of the box. After they had finished problem solving the students were asked to identify the group processes at work. They examined speaking patterns—who spoke frequently and was quiet and analyzed how these interactions affected the group. The goal was to prepare the student for the thinking processes they would need to structure an organization such as ODW and write the constitution. Jen wrote:

> Today was a perfect example of how these youth can handle the task set before them. Today was an education packed day full of activities and discussions. They proved themselves responsible, cooperative, organized, teachable and mature. (1999)

The following day was the bus trip to Philadelphia. Brian Atwood picked the Philly area as the place to do the drafting of the ODW Constitution because he wanted it to mirror the writing of the US Constitution. The day before the student delegates drafted the constitution they toured Independence Hall and visited the Liberty Bell. Mike remembered:

> We went all over the place. We had historical tours with guides who dressed the part. It was a lot of fun. I loved history as a kid. They wanted us to get inspired by the way the constitution was written in the US and then say ... here we are, we have all of these schools from all over the country and we are going to sit down and write our Constitution.

That evening the students met and were presented with a variety of structural models. A speaker from ODW Norway explained their organization's structure. Then Jen described the Michigan Community Foundation Youth Program's organizational plan. USAID shared other possible models from a range of programs.

Wednesday, July 21st began peacefully enough. The Mission Statement Committee presented their draft to the group. It was passed after some tweaking and discussion. In its final form it read:

> WE, the youth of the United States of America, strongly believe that every child deserves to choose his or her own path to success. We believe that knowledge

and understanding are maps that lead down these paths. Operation Day's Work strives for local, national and universal unity among all youth through, friendship, service and global financial support. After educating ourselves about our chosen project and culture, we work to raise funds for this cause.

We are "youth helping youth to help themselves." (Operation Day's Work, USA, 1999)

After lunch, all the facilitators and sponsors with the exception of Jen and Justin, another representative from a youth organization, were asked to leave the room by some of the young adult leaders. They wanted the students to decide on issues of structure and sponsorship without adult interference. Unfortunately, when the adults left, the group's carefully orchestrated harmony began to unravel. Jen wrote:

The group got in a big circle all across the room. It took them a half an hour to stop taking personal opinions and break up into their school groups and discuss ODW's structure. After an hour of working in their school groups, they came back together. Each school presented their idea for a structure. There was no facilitator though a gatekeeper was selected. It got very interesting, because soon the group was led by few high school delegates that took charge. Unfortunately, some of the other high school and middle school delegates felt overlooked and not able to state their opinions. No decision was made and soon it was dinner time. The group got worried about their progress and lack of unity, so they asked for help. (1999)

Beth remembered the meeting as.

Frustrating at times. Outspoken and authoritative kids got up and it was hard for everyone to get a voice. When it got heated, people would say that we were here for the same reasons; we were given guidelines; we had Norway as an example; we had been spoken to by representatives from Norway, so we had our model for a constitution.

Looking back, Mike felt part of the problem was the anti-American sentiments that surfaced when the adults left.

Some of students from Norway were kind of stuck up and they liked to talk badly about the United States. As a kid, I didn't have a great idea of what was going on in the world, or understand why people from other countries wouldn't like us too much. I do now. ... But I remember being really upset. I mean we had built a whole school in Pakistan. They should have shown us more respect.

Ron remembers meeting with the Broad Meadows delegation after that fateful afternoon. He said that the Broad Meadows students walked out of the meeting which had devolved into chaos. They described the meeting as a "shout fest" and expressed their anger at being ignored by the high school students who acted as if the middle school students had nothing to say.

Ron felt that the problem in part was that the ODW Norway program was geared toward high school students, as the focus of the fund-raising was working in a paid job for one day. Since US students cannot get working papers until age 14, the middle school students wanted to propose alternative methods of fund-raising and felt frustrated when these concerns and ideas were ignored or downplayed. Mary recalled, "When it got a little bit dicey … Mr. Adams took us out to give us time to think and plan so that we were prepared and wouldn't talk out of frustration or anger. He gave us practical advice about what we could do going forward."

Prior to coming to Philadelphia, the Broad Meadows students had developed a plan. They decided to advocate for a community service day that could take the place of a work day. The students would identify the types of services they could provide in their local communities. They would then create pledge sheets, like people do in breast cancer walks and collect money for each hour of service they performed. This way two communities would benefit: their local community and the community in which the project they had voted for was located. They were unable to present this plan at the meeting and worked with Ron to develop strategies so they could successful present their plan the next day. If it was accepted, they believed, it would create a structure where middle school students could play just as an important role in ODW as their high school peers.

That night student representatives from each school met during dinner to decide how to proceed. They met with the facilitators after dinner to develop a plan.

Thursday, July 22, began with an icebreaker activity. Students were divided into small groups by peer facilitators. Each group formed a circle and one student got into the middle and danced when music was played. All the students on the outside of the circle were asked to imitate the student's dance.

Next the students got into school groups and were asked to write down what they appreciated about their teachers, facilitators, and each of the schools present. These affirmations were shared with the group. Each school group then presented their ideas for the structure of ODW USA. The ideas were discussed and voted on. Broad Meadows' plan for a community service day as an alternative to a day's work was approved. After a long day of debate and discussion, a group of students volunteered to write the constitution that evening.

Friday, July 23, began with a "freeze game." Music was played and then students were told to freeze in a particular position when the music stopped. After the icebreaker, they engaged in another process discussion. They needed to decide whether a project, country, or theme should be the focus of the proposals solicited for the following year. The delegates decided to pick a country and they got into their school groups to a select a country that they presented to the groups. Two of the groups had delegates from the country they selected. They shared personal stories about the country. The personal nature of these presentations influenced the students and El Salvador was selected as the country they chose to help.

That afternoon the Constitutional Committee presented a draft of the ODW Constitution. The delegates discussed the draft and voted. The final document was signed using quill pens. The Convention ended with a debriefing session where students reflected upon what they had learned. Beth said:

> I do remember signing it with a quill pen. We got on line and it was a solemn line. We each took ours turns. It was momentous. There was a collective sense of accomplishment. We left realizing that we had done something remarkable. It was a really exciting experience for a middle school student.

ODW USA adopted the core philosophical principles of ODW Norway in is constitution. It is a democratic, student-run organization that embraces the concept of solidarity and supports projects that provide sustainable educational programs for youth. In keeping with this tradition the constitution states:

> To demonstrate our respect for those we hope to help, the Operation Day's Work committee in each member school will work to educate themselves, other students and their community about inequality of opportunity for youth in developing nations.

However, while the guiding principles are the same, the structure of ODW USA is less complex and more decentralized. According to the Constitution, the member school is the foundation of the organization. Each member school votes to select the annual project and develops its own educational program about the project and country that has been selected for funding. In addition, they make all of the decisions at the local level. The students determine the role of the ODW advisors, process for selecting student representatives, and the methods for keeping records.

The ODW Constitution calls for an annual convention where representatives of each school meet to decide upon a theme or country for the upcoming year and make any needed changes to the constitution. At the convention representatives also elect members to the National Committee.

The National Committee, initially outlined in the constitution, has 8 members, with one representative from each of the pilot schools. Members serve for one year. They make decisions that affect the overall organization. They solicit

NGO proposals for the country or theme that was chosen at the convention. They also determine the month in which the member schools can schedule their day or days of work.

The constitution also sets forth guidelines for ODW sponsorships. No donations will be accepted from corporations that produce alcohol, tobacco, firearms, and war supplies or destroy the environment. To be accepted as a sponsor the company must practice fair labor policies and cannot violate child labor laws.

Year 2—El Salvador

During its second year, the member schools voted upon proposals for projects in El Salvador. They selected a three-year training project for 300 youth orphaned or badly traumatized by the civil war in El Salvador. The project was implemented by the Salesian Mission and provided counseling, basic education, and vocational training.

Exit USAID

The following summer ODW held its second annual conference in Minneapolis, Minnesota. However, when George Bush took office in 2001, his administration made cuts in the USAID programs. ODW USA was one of the programs that was cut and the pilot schools were left without the funding provided by a national sponsor to develop ODW on their own.

CONCLUSION

Both The Kid's Campaign to Build a School for Iqbal and ODW enhance participants' global awareness. However, ODW's underlying premises and its overarching structure were developed outside the Broad Meadows school community. The program was brought to United States to promote global understanding. As stated in the introduction, it is ironic that this program which was devised in Norway during the 1960s and transported to the United States in the 1990s fosters 21st-century skills and global competencies that experts in the education community have identified as essential for American students to succeed and compete in the 21st century.

The framework for competency mentioned in the introduction was fully elaborated by the Council of Chief State School Officers and the Asia Society Partnership for Global Learning in their task force report (2011). They claim that globally competent students should be able to:

1. Investigate the world beyond their immediate environment, framing significant problems and conducting well-crafted and age appropriate research.
2. Recognize perspectives other than their own, articulating and explaining such perspectives thoughtfully and respectfully.
3. Communicate ideas effectively with diverse audiences, bridging geographic, linguistic, ideological, and cultural barriers.
4. Take action to improve conditions, viewing themselves as players in the world and participating reflectively. (Mansilla & Jackson, p. 11)

The Task Forces' conception of global competence clearly aligns with the philosophy and practice of ODW. By conceptualizing their work as solidarity as opposed to charity, ODW creates a context for investigating the world where multiple perspectives can be considered and respected and students can take action based upon the needs of their peers in the global south.

As stated previously, in addition to global competency, educational experts believe that American students need to develop 21st-century skills in order to solve the problems and compete for jobs in an increasingly globalized world. Advocates feel that skills such as critical thinking and problem solving, collaboration, creativity, and communication will be critical (Trilling, Fadel, & the Partnership for 21st Century Skills, 2009).

Harvard professor Tony Wagner (2008) identified seven "survival skills" that students need to master. Many of the skills he recommends are fostered through participation in The Kid's Campaign and ODW. These include critical thinking and problem solving, collaboration across networks, agility and adaptability, taking initiative, effective oral and written communication, accessing and analyzing information, and curiosity and imagination.

As the following chapters will demonstrate participants in the ODW community at Broad Meadows demonstrate the four global competencies and acquire many of the 21st-century skills advocated by Wagner. Despite the Bush Administration's decision to discontinue funding, the program at Broad Meadows continued to grow. Ron and the students built upon the democratic student-centered structure developed in the previous campaigns and developed strategies and structures unique to Broad Meadows ODW.

Ron continuously connected ODW to past campaigns, and emphasized the history and tradition of activism of Broad Meadows Middle School. The Iqbal story and campaign became central elements of the school's folklore and antichild labor advocacy remains a key component of the evolving community of practice.

Chapter 6

ODW USA: A Year in the Life, Part 1

Investigating the World and Preparing to Take Action

The mind is not a vessel to be filled, but a fire to be kindled.

—Plutarch

Veterans Only

Structuring ODW poses significant challenges. First off, the after school program is comprised of students from three grade levels: 6th, 7th, and 8th. Students can join at any point in their middle school career. In order to maintain the ODW community, there must be meaningful opportunities for participation for the returning students who are known as the "veterans" as well as for the newcomers who are referred to as "rookies" or "newbies." Basic educational activities must be provided for the rookies, while simultaneously allowing the veterans to demonstrate their expertise.

In order to develop maximum participation, the veterans meet and plan the recruitment strategies and the kick-off meeting for the new school year. At these meetings Ron typically praises the students' prior accomplishments, reinforces democratic practices learned the previous year, and works with them to develop ideas for recruiting students and planning the kick-off meeting. The following vignette describes a typical meeting:

On a sunny Friday afternoon in early September, sixteen students arrived at Mr. Adams room, to attend a "veteran's only" meeting. The meeting began with some cheerleading by Ron.

I want to tell you why I am here …. I am here because I think what you are doing is fantastic. I think it is important that you want to help your peers in other countries. I am here because you guys want to change the world and I am with you. As long as you are willing to give up Fridays, I am here. (Kids were quiet;

and smiled at the praise.) Last year ODW raised $26,000 to build seven group homes for AIDS orphans in Ethiopia. Broad Meadows Middle School raised $3,964 for this project.

Student 1, a pretty 8th-grade girl with curly auburn hair, spontaneously grabbed a picture from the counter and stood in the sink. (The oblong classroom once served as a science lab.) She held up the picture of one of the new group homes and described it. She handed it to another student who passed it around. Ron resumed speaking. He spoke about Selamta, the project in Ethiopia that they had sponsored the previous year. The project's goal was to build seven group homes for AIDS orphans and hire seven live-in foster moms and foster aunts to form a family unit for ten "siblings" who will live in each of the group homes. Ron said:

> Thousands of Ethiopian kids are living in warehouses. They are all AIDS orphans. Because of your work 70 of these orphans will be moved to group homes where a family structure will be created for them. They are between the ages of four and fourteen. What you did was more than raise money, you changed lives.

The kids were beaming. Ron seemed to sense it was time to begin work. He said, "Are you ready to begin planning for the New Year? How are you going to recruit rookies?"

A student suggested that they make posters with sign-up sheets to post in the cafeteria and other places. Another recommended that they write announcements that would become a part of the school's morning and afternoon announcements. A third thought they should visit "rookie home bases"—6th-grade homerooms.

Ron interjected, "It's hard for a group to make decisions. Why don't you pick a volunteer to write things on the board?"

One student volunteered to be scribe. Another took on the role of spokesperson. They decided upon four posters and four days of announcements.

Ron broke in, "Can you divide the tasks so that everyone who wants to participate gets a job? How can you do this fairly and democratically?"

A student said, "Let's put names in a hat." The other students concurred. A girl wearing a gray crocheted cap removed it from her head. She handed it to the spokesperson who said, "Who wants to do posters?" The students wrote their names on scraps of paper and a student picked four from the hat. They seemed pleased with the process and did the same for the announcements.

Ron stepped in again and said, "You have four days of announcements. Is there any way that you can do this so that many people are involved?"

A lively discussion followed. They decided that different people can make morning and afternoon announcements and two people can be involved in writing and delivering each announcement. They put all of the names back in the hat and selected partners randomly.

The discussion then turned to the first meeting day. What should we do with the rookies? Someone said, "Feed them."

Another said, "That's a bribe."

Someone else chimed in, "It's okay to bribe them on the first day."

This led to a fairly serious discussion about students' motivations for joining. There was concern that some students join for the wrong reasons. Some of the students claimed that some of their peers join for the food or because they want to go on trips. The students wanted them to understand the program's mission and join because they care about helping youth in the developing world.

They decided they should speak frankly with the "rookies" and work with Mr. Adams to develop a program to motivate them on the first day. The hat was passed around and volunteers submitted their names.

The meeting ended. An 8th-grade student waited for Ron. She had written an essay on Child Labor for the Oakseed International Essay Contest and won a $1,000 scholarship toward college. Ron was thrilled with the news and praised her highly. It was clearly a defining moment for them both!

The Official ODW Kick-off Meeting of the Year

The veterans spent the next two weeks implementing and refining their recruitment plan. They had additional planning meetings with Ron both before and after school. The end result was the kick-off meeting described in the vignette below. Here Ron introduced several of the themes that would frame the year's work and are essential for creating a community of practice. He used strategies that he had developed to build a team and create a sense of community.

It was 2:30 on a Friday in the middle of September. The bell rang and middle school students surged into the hallways. The decibel level increased dramatically. Short little boys who looked like they could still be in elementary school and tall gangly girls in varying stages of puberty filled the corridors and began walking toward the exit.

A group of students hovered in the hallway in front of Ron's classroom, room 109. They congregated in sex-segregated groups and seemed a bit uneasy. Ron walked in and asked six 8th graders, ODW veterans, to go to the cafeteria to set up. Ron said that he had 55 students sign up and 40 of the sign-ups had shown up. The group was so large that he could not hold the meeting in his room. He moved among the students and began to reveal the meeting's first theme: team building. He said:

You will be going to the cafeteria. There will only be five tables. You must sit at
a table with students you don't know. This is okay. Today you might be strang-
ers, but you will become a team.

They moved en masse to the cafeteria. Several of the veterans approached
the rookies. They shepherded them to tables where they joined them: two
veterans at each table. The room filled with the sounds of forty plus preado-
lescents talking and laughing simultaneously. It felt loud, and as if it could
get out of control at any minute.

Ron walked to the center of the cafeteria and held up his hand. He said the
word hands, softly, yet firmly and gave a hand signal. The noise went down
a decibel.

He said hands again, louder and with conviction. A number of students
looked up, raised their hands, and the decibel level went down dramatically.

One more hands and everyone was at attention. Ron looked around and
said:

A lot of big hearted people are here today. They are sixth, seventh and eighth
graders. You might not know everyone; but you are all here because you want
to help other kids around the world. Our goal is to become a team over the next
year. One way for you to get to know each other is to share food.

At the front of the cafeteria the veterans were setting up food. There was
quite a spread, fruit juices, potato chips, popcorn. They began to distribute it.
Ron continued:

The other students brought food for you. The PTO (Parent/Teacher's Organization) and the principal also donated food. The reason they donate the food is
that they are proud of what you do. They are proud of ODW and that you are
working to help kids in other countries.

The students happily snacked away. It was a diverse group; more girls than
boys, but more boys than in previous years. It was more racially diverse as
well. There were more black students. White and Asian students had been
the main groups in the past. One girl, new to the program, was wearing a
traditional Muslim dress and a *hijab*. When the students finished eating Ron
said:

You must now move to the auditorium. You must sit in the first four rows at the
center. You sit together because you are a team and by sitting together you will
feel like a team.

The veterans shepherded the rookies to the auditorium and ushered them
to their seats. Two 8th-grade veterans, a short boy and a tall gangly girl, took

turns leading the group. The boy asked everyone in the first row to rise, turn around, face the others, and introduce themselves.

The girl at the far end of the row began, "I am in in 8th grade and I have been in ODW since 6th grade. (She pointed to Ron). He is a great teacher." Everyone clapped.

The next student said, "I am in the 6th grade and this is my first year in ODW." Everyone clapped again.

Ron interjected, "We are a team, so after each person is done, let's see if we can clap in unison."

They tried this and he praised them. After each person spoke, they clapped and he reinforced the unity of the clap.

A student introduced herself loudly and with force. Ron said, "I like the power in your voice. Bring this power to speak for those who lack power."

After all of the students had introduced themselves, two alumni who were in high school arrived. They introduced themselves to the group.

The boy veteran who had been leading the group brought out the ODW mascot, Ducky, a huge stuffed duck wearing an ODW T-shirt, and introduced him to the group. The student leader was also wearing the official ODW shirt. He told the group, "I want to show you this t-shirt. On the back is a list of all the countries we have helped." He turned around and the other veteran leader slowly read off the list.

1999—Haiti
2000—El Salvador
2001—Nepal and US orphans of 9/11
2002—Ethiopia
2003—Bangladesh
2004—Sierra Leone
2005—Vietnam
2006—Rwanda
2007—Ethiopia

Another student stood up. He said, "The shirt is a banner that shows how much we can do. I hope that in a few years, the writing will be so small because of all of the people that we have helped."

Next they showed the students a video about the birth of ODW. It began with the Broad Meadows students winning the Reebok award for building the School for Iqbal and narrated the Iqbal story.

When the film ended several of the rookies wanted to know more about child labor. Mr. Adams and the veterans fielded their questions. Then meeting came to an end. As the students were leaving a group of veterans came over to Ron to share ideas. More ODW alumni arrived and they hung out with each other. It was a safe space to return to during the first month of High School.

WORLD CLASS: SIMULATION TO PROMOTE GLOBAL EMPATHY AND AWARENESS

After the rookies have decided to join ODW, they receive informal training to enhance their understanding of global issues affecting youth. Given the age and inexperience of the students Ron employs experiential learning to introduce the subject. He uses a simulation game, World Class that was developed by Net Aid, a nonprofit organization committed to ending extreme poverty around the world.

World Class is a role-play geared toward students aged 8 to 14. The purpose of the game is to help students understand how difficult it can be for youth living in dire poverty to remain in school and achieve their dreams. The game is based upon the lives of real children in Tamil Nadu, India, where Net Aid runs a world school house project.

Fifty student showed up for the next meeting. Ron ushered them to the gym. The veterans setup and doled out the snacks. One of the 8th graders whispered to Ron conspiratorially, "Is this the day we do the guilt trip?"

Before the game started, the students were told that they would take on the roles of actual children in Tamil Nadu, India. They were each given a set of cards that described the child's life situation and the child's dream for a future career. In order to win the game, the student must accumulate enough years of education to achieve his/her dream.

The kids took turns spinning the wheel and random events: a family illness, loss of parental job, a drought, or a flood could force a child to leave school for a period of time and take on the role of caregiver or "breadwinner" at a menial job (National Peace Corps Association, 2003, p. 11). By the end of the game only two of the students were able to garner enough years of schooling to achieve their dreams.

After the game was finished Ron debriefed the students and asked them what they had learned:

> *Sixth grade girl:* My person was a kid who had to make bricks all day and his parents didn't work. I felt bad because it wasn't really a game. It was real life for her.

> *Seventh grade boy:* I thought it was amazing how we, (Americans) just take things for granted, like having shoes.

> *Eighth grade girl:* Life is hard if you are poor and you are a girl. Most of the girls ended leaving school to help at home. Their dreams weren't taken as seriously as the boy's dreams.

As the students were leaving the meeting an Asian girl in the 7th grade came up to Ron and said, "If my family didn't move, I could have been a face on a card.

During the week Ron sent the students an e-mail reinforcing their experience. He said:

> Last meeting we learned about Iqbal Masih's stolen childhood and abusive life as a child slave. We discovered there are millions of children like Iqbal in many countries. At this meeting we learned about what daily life is like for some of those children. It was sad to see their dreams evaporating because of lack of education. At this meeting we developed "empathy," not pity for children who struggle to get into schools.
>
> At this meeting, we became more dedicated to helping some children in some country during this school year. Given a chance, those children's hopes and dreams might blossom. A chance ... that's what ODW delivers—that, and hope.

In addition, Ron included a copy of an e-mail that he had received from an education student in New Zealand.

> Dear Ron,
>
> We are third year students at Auckland University who are studying to become primary school teachers. We read about Operation Day's Work. We found your work very inspirational and hope that when we have our own classes that our students will have the same motivation and enthusiasm. We have discussed and are interested in how we will make an impact on our students about social issues.
>
> Katie, Sylvie and Lisa. (E-mail from Ron Adams, September 27, 2008)

Researching Global Inequality

The next session builds upon the empathy developed in the game, by having the students engage in research on world poverty. The veterans take on a teaching/mentoring role in this session as they help the students conduct research that they had done themselves as rookies in previous years. A synopsis of the meeting and the teaching technique used follows:

Another sunny afternoon and forty-two students crammed into room 109. Eighth graders distributed juice and snacks. A small Staples whiteboard was propped in front of the blackboard. The meeting's agenda was written in bold multicolored markers:

I.   Game
II. Research
III. PowerPoint

Ron focused on the group and said, "This is the agenda you came up with." The students began by rehashing their feelings about the game they played the previous week. After they finished Ron said:

You have been very respectful of the kids you have been role playing. But now it is time to take it to the next level. The question we are going to research today is—What is the state of the World's children?

The students moved to the cafeteria where a large map was posted on the wall. A mobile blackboard with different colored chalk stood near the map. The students were seated in tables in groups of six with two veterans per table. Each student received a copy of the 2006 edition of Junior Scholastic's *The World in Focus: Fast Facts on 194 Countries.* The veterans served as tutor/mentors. Their role was to teach the rookies how to find the information needed for the research activity. Ron asked what information they needed to find. The veterans provided the answers.

Literacy rates of total population; comparison between males and females
Life expectancy of total population; comparison between male and females
Gross Domestic Product (GDP); total wealth divided by total population.

As the students provided the categories he asked the veterans to help the rookies find the information for the United States. He wrote categories and data on the mobile blackboard.

Then he introduced a new concept, the Human Development Index or HDI, and the following student/teacher exchange occurred:

Ron: HDI describes a country's quality of life; its economic and human well-being. It combines life expectancy literacy and purchasing power into one number. It is done on a scale of 0-1... For example, if you were taking a science test, what grade would you want to get?

Student: 100

Ron: What would you consider a good grade?

Student: 95%

Ron: On the HDI that would read 0.95 for the quality of life. But what if you received a 0.40? What would that mean?

Student: You failed.

Ron: What if the quality of life was 0.20? If that was your grade?

The students moaned and made faces. Nobody said anything.

Ron: Sometimes the HDI is called the misery index because so many countries get a failing grade.

Each table was given an area of the world to research and a sticker with a blue dot. The group had to research their area of the world and then decide

Table 6.1 Students' Research Findings

Area of the world		North America	South America	Africa	Europe	Asia	Oceania
Country	USA	Haiti	Bolivia	Somalia	Moldova	Afghanistan	Kiribati
GDP	$41,000	$1,700	$2,900	$600	$1,800	$800	$800
Literacy rate, M/F	99/99	55/51	93/82	50/26	99/99	51/21	n/a
Life expectancy, M/F	79/80	51/54	62/66	46/50	65/72	41/42	58/64
HDI	0.94	0.47	0.68	n/a	0.67	n/a	n/a

which countries were most in need of help. Students were allowed to dissent from the group as long as they could back up their decisions with evidence. Once the group had decided, one member placed a blue dot on the map and another wrote the statistics on the mobile blackboard.

Lively discussions ensued. Intermittently, students got up from their tables and moved to the front of the cafeteria and studied the wall map. By the end of the activity, the following information had been placed on the blackboard (Junior Scholastic, 2006).

The students presented their findings. They were somber and seemed shocked by the variations in the statistics. They were especially troubled by the differences in life expectancies that they believe is a consequence of economic inequality.

Ron told them that in the coming weeks they can research agencies that serve youth in these world areas and invite them to submit proposals to ODW. They can also begin planning ways to raise money and awareness for whatever program the participating ODW schools select.

The students returned to Ron's room to view a PowerPoint about ODW that was made by a group of the veterans. The students discussed and critiqued the PowerPoint. Then the meeting was adjourned.

Raising Funds and Awareness

The next meeting took place on a rainy overcast day. There were fewer students this week—around thirty. There was an agenda on the board in front of the room. The veterans took charge of distributing the juice and snacks. Ron walked over and whispered to me. "This is when the 8th graders become the leaders. The goal is to shift power to the students. It's a goal. We might get there by November or by March. It's different every year."

Ron called the meeting to order and introduced the veterans who ran the meeting. The first item on the agenda was fund-raising ideas. One student led the meeting by calling on different students while another wrote their ideas on the board. The list included new ideas as well as ideas that had worked successfully in the past:

Talent Show
Dance
Penny Power
Hot Cocoa sale
Raffle
Sell decorated cookies around the holiday
Garage sale

One of the 8th graders, Rebecca, contacted the manager of a local restaurant, the Chateau, about doing an ODW fund-raiser. The manager said he would consider an ODW night where 20% of the restaurant's proceeds would go to ODW.

The students excitedly discussed the pros and cons of the ideas. Ron jumped in intermittently. When the students went off on tangents, he brought them back on task and then deferred to the student leaders. The students wanted to do all of the fund-raisers. Ron laughed and said, "My head is spinning! Where do you want to start?" They decided on the restaurant night. The young woman who knew the restaurant manager promised to contact him again and report back.

The second item on the agenda was "Spreading the Word." Ron told the students that Rita, a former ODW leader who was a student at the University of Massachusetts, Dartmouth, wanted to invite a small team from ODW Broad Meadows to speak at the university's Oxfam Hunger Banquet. The students then had to decide who will serve as spokespersons for ODW. Veterans were nominated, their credential enumerated, and a vote followed. The three students who were selected decided to work on their presentation and scheduled a meeting before school with Mr. Adams for help with fine-tuning. After the presentation, which took place three weeks later, the students were presented with $100 donation to ODW from the Rotar Act service Club at UMass, Dartmouth.

Subsequent Meetings

The next meetings followed a similar pattern. The Chateau Restaurant formally agreed to sponsor the fund-raiser: on a Thursday. Each patron needed to present a coupon, and then 20% of the check for lunch, dinner, or take-out orders would be donated to ODW. The students had to decide how to organize and spread the word about the event.

The 8th-grade student leaders took charge of the meeting. This time there was a moderator, a recorder, who wrote the ideas on the board, and a note taker, who took meeting minutes. The students decided on the first Thursday in December and came up with a list of advertising ideas:

Design posters
Broadcast the event as part of the school's morning and afternoon announcements
Advertisement on the restaurant website
Newspaper
School and other community websites

With prompting from Ron, the students figured out democratic practices to form committees to work on these ideas. Ron let them develop their own rules as long as the committees were mixed by grades. Part of the ODW ethos is that the veterans are always mentoring future ODW leaders.

This ethos was reinforced by the next event on the agenda. A veteran and a team of rookies presented a two-sided poster that they developed on last year's project in Ethiopia. Their teammates seemed interested and were supportive of their efforts.

Fund-raising ideas can come from inside the group as well as from alumni. Just as Rita organized a speaking engagement one year (2007), another alumna Mai, a sophomore at Syracuse University in New York, proposed a Mary Kay Cosmetics fund-raiser another year (2009). Before accepting the proposal, the ODW members decided to investigate the company. Three teams researched Mary Kay online and reported their findings to their peers. They found that Mary Kay has no animal testing; makes donations to the Red Cross, programs to end domestic violence and breast cancer research. Most importantly to the students, Mary Kay has a posted code of ethics and does not use child labor.

The students voted to do the Mary Kay fund-raiser, if Mai could obtain a second source that confirmed that Mary Kay does not use child labor and if she could find out if the ingredients on the beauty products were clearly listed so that people with allergies will not have problems. A true ODW alumna, Mai obtained the information the students requested and the students embarked upon the fund-raiser. They brought home order forms and asked their parents to purchase cosmetics and to bring order forms to their places of work. Thirty-six students participated in the fund-raiser. They raised $800.00. Twenty-five percent of the sales, or $200, was donated to ODW. Mai Phan traveled down from Syracuse to attend the ODW meeting and deliver the cosmetics herself.

The meetings devoted to general education and brainstorming are prelude to the main event—selecting a project for the coming year. As with the other key educational components, Ron provides the structure for the students to develop the skills needed to read and analyze a grant proposal.

Bricks and Bouquets: The Grant Application Process

Grants applications are due by October 31st each year. Proposals are short and limited to five pages. The grant application, which is available on the ODW website, delineates the information that the organization needs to provide. There are seven basic informational categories that the middle school students need to read and evaluate.

The first category is project information. This provides the students with basic contact information for the organization as well as the name of the project director, project start and end dates, and the amount requested. The second category is organizational background. This includes a brief history of the organization as well as a collaborative history between the American-based organization and the partner NGO in the country where the project will take place. Applicants are also asked to describe their prior experiences in the area proposed by the project.

The next section of the application, project description, focuses upon the project itself. The applicants are asked to describe the project's goal, rationale, and delineate its objectives in measureable terms. The fourth section focuses upon project beneficiaries. Applicants are asked to explain who will benefit and provide specifics such as potential beneficiaries' economic status, gender, and geographical location. They must also explain how they will benefit and if the youth themselves will be involved with the planning and implementation of the project.

Project implementation and evaluation follow. Applicants must describe major activities and explain who, when, where, and how these activities will be carried out. They are also asked to address sustainability. In other words, they must explain how they will continue the project once the grant money has been spent. Applicants must also explain how they will evaluate the project's success and include information on the types of data and the methods they will use to collect it.

The final section is the proposed project budget. Applicants must describe other resources the organization will contribute to the project. These can include other financial, in-kind, or human resources. The proposal stipulates that no more than 10% of the funds be used for administrative costs (Operation Day's Work, 2014).

While the application may seem straightforward to the adult reader, a grant proposal is a new and challenging type of reading for 6th, 7th, and 8th graders. As a consequence, learning how to interpret this type of document becomes a communal effort and Ron has developed strategies to effectively guide middle school students through the process.

Reviewing the Proposals

Once the grant applications have been submitted, the students are divided into groups. Each group is provided with a multiple copies of a single proposal to review. They begin by researching the organizations that submitted the proposal. They use web-based charity evaluators such as charity navigator and guide star to gain information on the charity's overall rating, finances, and accountability. They also refer to Junior Scholastic's *World in Focus: Fast Facts on 194 Countries* to determine the GDP, HDI, life expectancy, and literacy rates of the countries where the projects have been proposed.

Students are then given a week to review their proposals. They are encouraged to go over the proposal with family members and friends. When they read the proposal they are asked to keep the following questions in mind:

1. How many lives will the project change?
2. Is the plan sustainable? How will agency continue the project once the ODW money has been spent?
3. What are the strengths of the proposal?
4. What are the weaknesses? What worries you?

Each group makes a poster of their proposal's three greatest strengths (Bouquets) and three greatest weaknesses (Bricks). These Bouquets and Bricks are listed side by side. At the following meeting the students present their posters to the entire group and discuss the proposed projects.

In the 2008–2009 school year, ODW received 7 proposals from the following organizations:

Alliance for Children: Develop a computer Lab with 12 computers

Zambia   GDP: 1,000;   Life Expectancy: 38/37   HDI: 0.39   Literacy Rate: 87/75
CHABHA: Construct a five-room building for community's needs including classes for orphans and other youth
(Children affected by HIV/AIDS)
GDP: 1,600   Life Expectancy: 47/48

Rwanda   HDI: 0.45   Literacy Rate: 76/65
Heritance: Teach Kenyan history through field trips to make youth proud of being Kenyan

Kenya   GDP: 1,200   Life Expectancy: 53/53   HDI: 0.47   Literacy Rate:
    91/80
Lwala: Develop a community technology center which teaches health and
    technology.

Kenya   GDP: 1,200   Life Expectancy: 53/53   HDI: 0.47   Literacy Rate:
    91/80
Partners in Health: Help 535 children with HIV/AIDS and teach other chil-
    dren how not to get AIDS.
Rwanda   GDP: 1,600   Life Expectancy: 47/48   HDI: 0.45   Literacy
    Rate: 76/65
Sabre Books Project: Donate 20,000 books and some furniture. 800 of the
    books deal with AIDS prevention

Sierra Leone   GDP: 900   Life Expectancy: 48/49   HDI: 0.29   Literacy
    Rate: 40/21
Village Health Works: Develop a community health center for 20,000 people
    (see 50 patients a day). Reduce malaria by 85% and increase life expec-
    tancy, provide   services for community members with HIV/AIDS

Burundi   GDP: 700   Life Expectancy: 44/45   HDI: 0.37   Literacy Rate:
    59/45

The students presented their posters in mid-November. Two groups presented
and Ron paraphrased what the students said in a summary form. Then students discussed the projects. They used the criteria that Ron had outlined and
added their own interpretations. They were very serious and thoughtful about
presenting and evaluating the proposals.

During the discussion, the majority of the students felt that the book project
in Sierra Leone had more Bricks than Bouquets. They believed that cost of
shipping of 20,000 books and furniture would eat up the funds and questioned
if this would be the best use of the money. They were also skeptical about
the Kenyan history project. While they felt that going on field trips to learn
Kenyan history could increase student pride and awareness, they did not think
that this would have as much of a life-changing effect as some of the other
projects.

The students saw the value of the computer projects as they realized how
important it is to be tech-savvy in the global economy. The Zambia project's
goal was to purchase 12 computers and hire a teacher to provide instruction
in use of word and the Internet, so that students who took part in the program
would be computer literate by the time they reached 9th grade. The Broad
Meadows students thought this was a worthwhile goal and that in addition
Zambian students could use the computers to communicate with kids in other

countries. One of the poster presenters pointed out that the agency Alliance for Children had an excellent track record with this kind of project. However, she was concerned about the low teacher's salary—$4,000 a year.

The students felt that the project to develop the center to teach technology and health also had many positives. They especially liked the idea that while the teacher would oversee the program, youth who had received training would actually run the center's day-to-day operations. However, one of the presenters pointed out that the proposal was vague in important areas, for example, it did not specify how many computers would be needed to make the program a success.

While Broad Meadows students felt technology was important several argued that the health-related projects addressed more pressing needs. They saw the CHABHA project and the Partners in Health project as having a similar focus—helping youth with HIV/AIDS in Rwanda. The students thought both were good projects. However, they felt that CHABHA needed the ODW funding more. The Partners in Health project already had $45,000 earmarked for the project and the ODW money would be used to expand the existing project. The CHABHA project needed the ODW money to begin. CHABHA wanted to construct a five-room building that would service 2,500 people. The building would become a center where HIV testing, counseling, and prevention workshops could take place.

The students who presented the Burundi project to assist in the further development of a community health clinic felt that this project had great potential for changing people's lives. The clinic is located in the Kigutu region, which is one of the most remote and poorest areas of the country where there are no other health services available. The region has high rates of HIV/AIDS, malaria, typhoid, and other diseases. The students pointed out that one of the clinic's goals was to reduce the malaria death rate by 85% by providing families with insecticide-treated nets. They also wanted to provide services and medicines to individuals infected with HIV/AIDS. The students felt that these services could expand life expectancy and really make a difference in the area.

After the presentations were completed the students had a week to decide. The posters were kept on display in the cafeteria, so the students could revisit them. Students were allowed to lobby for a specific project if they felt strongly about it. At the next meeting, students cast a secret ballot for the project they hoped to sponsor. The votes were tallied and each school's final vote was sent to the ODW coordinator. Each year, the project that receives the most school votes becomes the ODW project of the year.

The proposal to build the clinic in Burundi obtained the most votes at Broad Meadows and the other ODW schools. Together, all of the schools raised $26,000 to make that project a reality.

CHILD LABOR-FREE SHOPPING TRIP:
SHOPPING WITH A CONSCIENCE

Planning and Preparation

On the Wednesday before Thanksgiving, members of Broad Meadows ODW board a Peter Pan bus for South Shore Plaza, the local mall in the neighboring community of Braintree. Their goal is to interview store managers to determine if child labor is used to produce the merchandise and/or food they sell in their store and ask them to produce a worker's code of conduct to guarantee that the products are child labor free.

In order to prepare for the trip the students obtain a list of all of the stores in the mall. The stores are divided into two categories: superstores with a known history of child labor like the GAP, Disney, Abercrombie & Fitch, and Nike and regular stores. The names of all of the stores are written on index cards. Students are divided into small groups that include both veterans and rookies. The cards are placed in a hat. First, the teams select a superstore. Then, they take turns randomly selecting cards for other stores.

The students are shown sample worker codes of conduct from stores such as Eddie Bauer, Reebok, and IKEA. Passages like the following from Eddie Bauer are provided as examples:

Eddie Bauer's Factory Workplace Code of Conduct

Eddie Bauer is committed to providing customers with the highest quality and value in our products. We believe this commitment is met in part through strong relationships with our associates and by selecting business partners who share our commitment to ethical practices and agree to our standards of business conduct. The following conditions are required for factories producing our products:

Forced Labor

There shall not be any use of forced labor, whether in the form of prison labor, indentured labor, bonded labor or otherwise.

Child Labor

No person shall be employed at an age younger than 15 (or 14 where the law of the country of manufacture allows) or younger than the age for completing compulsory education in the country of manufacture where such age is higher than 15. ("Global labor practice: Company information Eddie Bauer," 2015)

Veterans talk with rookies about what to say and do and they provide them following student-prepared script to refer to if they feel nervous: "Hello, I'd like to buy your clothes/food/accessories, but first I need to know, if your store use child labor to make its clothes/food/accessories? Is everything you make guaranteed child labor free?" (ODW, 2007). After they ask these questions or whenever they feel comfortable, they can request to see the worker's code of conduct.

The students are also provided with cards printed by the Child Labor Coalition and given to interested schools or individuals. The card is blank on one side. The students write antichild labor messages and a request that the store manager send proof that their store's merchandise or food was not produced by child labor to ODW USA. On the other side, there is a Child Labor Coalition photo of a child at a sewing machine. That side has the Child Labor Coalition contact information and introduces the cardholder as a Child Labor Coalition antichild labor activist. Students also write the contact information for ODW USA and sign their names. They leave the cards with store managers who are not able to provide the workers' code of conduct at the time of the store interview and ask them to send this information (Adams, 2007; ODW Broad Meadows, 2004).

Findings, Reactions, and Reflections

After the shopping trip, each student group prepares a list of the stores they visited and writes a brief synopsis (a sentence or two) about what happened. They e-mail their responses to Ron. He puts together a packet for the following meeting's debriefing session. The following list compiled by group # 2 in 2007 is a typical example of a student list:

- Radio shack: The manager was nice, but he did not know. No code of conduct!
- Michael's place: Could not get anybody. Manager came when we left!
- Talbot's accessories and shoes: Manager was an absolute jerk who threw the card away when we started leaving. As we left the manager said, "hahahahahahaha"!
- (Just kidding about the smile)
- Lander jewelers: Threw away the card in our face! Never gave an answer. Beat around the bush.
- CVS: Didn't want to deal with us. Made up vacation story.

At the 2007 debriefing meeting, the students enthusiastically reflected upon what they had learned. They were most troubled by the fact that the majority of the 100 store managers interviewed did not know whether or not their merchandise was produced by child labor. Several did not know what child labor was. ODW students reflected upon what they had learned:

Student 1: "The managers truly didn't know, or corporate HQ said they could not tell."

Student 2: "They should know because they own or run the store."

Student 3: "I wished they actually had proof, like a Workers' Code of Conduct stating that they didn't use child labor."

Student 4: "I wish that they could take attitude adjustment lessons because some managers were really rude."

Student 5: "I learned that I don't get intimidated by adults, and I let them know that I am not just some cute, little kid asking a silly question. I mean business."

Student 6: "I learned child labor is closer than we think. Some of my favorite stores could be using children to make clothes."

Student 7: "I learned that I live in a world where people don't know what they are buying."

The students found the attitude of the GAP employees the most frustrating to deal with as they simply refused to talk about it. They said they weren't permitted to discuss this issue.

As usual Ron reinforced the students' work in a follow-up e-mail. He both described their work and praised their effort:

Thanks to the grade 8 veterans who demonstrated quiet strength and leadership. The vets organized the groups, the lists of stores to visit, led the way, lifting rookies along the way.

Wow! What a day. The echoes of your questions are still rippling in the stores you visited today. Well done, everyone! (2007)

When the students return from Thanksgiving break the focus shifts from broad global concerns to working to make the project they have selected a reality and in the process they learn how to change the world for the better in their own small way.

CONCLUSION

The initial meetings lay the foundation for the ODW community for the school year. According to Wenger (1998), the structure of a community of practice consists of three elements: mutual engagement, joint enterprise, and shared repertoire. Mutual engagement refers to types of interaction that shape the culture and practice of the group. The group's unifying purpose and goal; its reason for being lays the foundation for the community's joint enterprise. Mutual engagement and joint enterprise are in a constant state of flux as the manner of interaction and the enterprise itself are constantly being negotiated by community members.

Shared repertoire refers to cultural resources produced and maintained by the community over time. These resources include routines, tools, and ways of doing things, stories, gestures, and actions. These activities and artifacts develop literal and symbolic meaning and through a shared history helps to create a sense of identity and belonging to the community and the larger world to which it connects (pp. 73–85).

At the opening meeting students are introduced to the Iqbal story, The Kid's Campaign, and the "heroic kids" of Broad Meadows who founded ODW. They see the kids who came before them on film and hear the testimonials of the veterans during the introductory activity. They also meet and hear the stories of ODW veterans who are in high school or college and have returned to visit. As the year progresses these stories are revisited and retold repeatedly.

Another mechanism for reinforcing group identity is speaking in unison. This technique is the foundation of the "ODW greeting." Whenever a visitor or a prospective student member comes to a meeting, the students raise their hands, palms out flat, and move them in a semicircle counterclockwise. They say hi and the person's name in unison while making this gesture. The knowledge of the greeting signifies insider status, yet the action itself creates a welcoming environment. (As a recipient of the greeting over the years, I experienced its welcoming effect.)

Sharing food and snacking carry literal and symbolic meaning. The food is seen as reward for their good deeds. It is donated by various individuals or groups, the principal, the PTO, parents and signifies that the participants' actions and the participants themselves are special.

Ducky, the ODW mascot, is a constant presence. It is not uncommon to enter an ODW meeting and see a middle schooler sitting on a counter top hugging the huge stuffed duck wearing an ODW shirt while discussing AIDS victims in Africa or child labor in Nepal. To the outside observer, this serves as a reminder that these are children discussing serious social problems.

ODW T-shirts also have a symbolic significance. During the introductory session the veteran student referred to it as "a banner that shows how much we can do." The story behind the T-shirt, as well as the annual T-shirt ceremony will be explored in the next chapter.

The two weeks of educational activities further shape the culture of ODW, Broad Meadows and forge a sense of purpose. They provide meaningful experiences for newcomers on the periphery and create a shared experience that becomes part of the community's repertoire. Veterans often say that the experience of "playing the game" (participating in the world-class simulation) changes for them over time and its meaning acquires more depth with repetition.

During the research activity the veterans take on the role of teacher/mentor. This allows them to show their expertise and serves as segue to the next meeting when they take on the leadership roles and begin to run the meetings. The Junior Scholastic publication *Fast Facts: the World in Focus* becomes a tool that is part of their shared repertoire. Participants use it to help them evaluate grant proposals.

The rituals surroundings the analysis of the grant application are critical practices that become part of the community's shared repertoire and enhance the students' identities as participants with a common goal. The buildup to this event provides the purpose and the intrinsic motivation for learning the complex set of skills needed to evaluate grant proposals.

The child labor-free shopping trip to the mall is a culminating event that reinforces the participants' connection to the shared history of child labor activism at Broad Meadows. Veterans assist the rookies and the experience helps them forge their own identities as global citizens and full members of the ODW community.

The development of the ODW as a community of practice leads to the growth of global competence and 21st century in a fluid informal educational setting. During the first three months of the program the students investigate the world beyond their immediate environment through participating in simulations, research, proposal evaluations, and a child labor-free shopping trip to the mall. These same activities help them to recognize perspectives other than their own and communicate ideas effectively. By beginning to plan and participate in fund-raising activities, vote upon a proposal, and participate in the child labor-free shopping trip to the mall they are taking action.

Many of the 21st-century skills advocated by Tony Wagner (2008) are practices developed through participation in ODW. Students engage in critical thinking, problem solving, and collaboration when designing and implementing a "rookie" recruitment campaign or running an ODW meeting. They must analyze and assess information, think critically, problem solve, collaborate, and communicate effectively when conducting research on global inequality, assessing grant proposals, and participating in the child labor-free shopping trip to the mall. They further develop these skills and competencies when they return from Thanksgiving break and begin to focus on learning, fund-raising, and raising awareness about the project they have selected for the year's campaign.

Chapter 7

A Year in the Life, Part 2

Making the Project of the Year a Reality

Education isn't preparation for life; education is life itself.

—John Dewey

The remainder of the school year is dedicated to self-education: learning about the project, raising awareness, educating others about ODW and the annual project and fund-raising. Fund-raising and raising awareness are often intertwined at ODW events. Events fall into three categories: annual events; one-time events that are initiated by students, staff, or alumni; and events geared to educating the ODW community itself. While the annual project is usually the focus of the community's joint enterprise, at times of crisis, such as 9/11, the Haitian Earthquake, and the Boston Marathon bombing, the group has voted to add a second project and events to its annual agenda. Regardless of how full the community's agenda becomes, the year ends with the day's work and the annual T-shirt ceremony, two cornerstones of the community's culture.

Annual Events

Over the years, several successful events have become part of the shared repertoire and have become annual rituals. Veterans had positive experiences with these events as rookies and as a consequence, share stories and suggest them during brainstorming sessions at meetings. Once ideas are suggested, student committees are formed to develop the events. Veterans and rookies are included in each committee. Thus the rookies are mentored by the veterans and learn how to organize events. It becomes a form of apprenticeship where ODW fund-raising ideas and events become rituals that are passed on from one group to the next. Perhaps nowhere is this process more evident than in the annual hot cocoa sale.

Hot Cocoa Sale

Every year during the third week in January, ODW sponsors a Hot Cocoa sale. In keeping with the spirit of the child labor-free shopping trip, ODW only sells cocoa that has been fair trade certified, guaranteed child labor free, and environmentally sustainable.

The students research fair trade cocoa on the Internet and contact the local Trader Joe's, which donates the fair trade cocoa for the annual event.

During the meeting prior to the sale, the students decorate Styrofoam cups for the cocoa. They include information on ODW, the annual project, child labor, and fair trade. Their goal is to educate their peers and raise money. As the students work, Ron walks around the room, reading their cups and cheering them on. He praises their designs and shows them to everyone in the room. As the meeting comes to an end, the students form a Styrofoam cup pyramid with the decorated cups on a table at the front of the room. Ron has the students surround the pyramid and takes pictures which he sends to the group.

The cup ceremony can be touching or comic. One year, one of the students decided to blow on the cup pyramid to see what would happen. The pyramid collapsed and the cups went flying around the room.

Irrespective of the cup ceremony's success, on Monday morning, an ODW volunteer team comprised of one veteran and two rookies arrives at the school cafeteria at 7:30 am to prepare and sell the hot cocoa and talk about the annual project. The hot cocoa sale continues from 7:30 to 8:30 a.m. throughout the entire week. Different veteran/rookie teams cover each day. The students generally raise between $50 and $60 for the annual project.

Penny Power

Penny Power is a popular fund-raiser that many ODW participants say is a favorite. It takes place on an annual basis at the end of March/beginning of April. Penny Power is a contest between the 6th, 7th, and 8th grades at Broad Meadows. Each grade has a large jar which is placed in the school cafeteria. Students bring in pennies and other forms of currency and whichever grade gets the most points wins.

The competition comes with the point system. Every penny in the grade's jar counts as a point. However, every other coin or bill in the grade's jar count as negative points. If someone puts a dollar in the jar the grade loses 100 points. The competition takes place at lunch time every day for a week. In order to increase the competition between the grades the money is counted each day by ODW volunteers from each grade and the winner for the day is announced during the morning announcements the next day. In addition, daily results are posted on a large "Results" poster board that hangs in the cafeteria next to the cashiers. Ron said:

> When a grade finishes last on Monday, there is usually a comeback effort the next day. If a grade wins a day, they tend to want to hold the lead, and they tend to surge the next day. No one wants to be average, so the team in the middle tends to rally the next day. Momentum builds daily as the results are announced and posted in the cafeteria. Kids talk it up and strategies are devised.
>
> Counting it up is an amazing experience to witness. The last day's jars are usually full due to the popular strategy of "dumping bills" into the leading grade's jar. On the last day ODW volunteers stay after school to count it all up and determine which grade won the competition and the title of, "The Year's Most Generous Grade."

Before the Penny Power competition begins, a committee of ODW students create a PowerPoint presentation showing photos of the youth the annual ODW project is geared to help. The photographs are supplied by the partner NGO. When the winner of the competition is announced the PowerPoint is shown in the cafeteria on the high-definition monitor. The goal is to show the students that youth like themselves will benefit as a result of the competition. Penny Power is a very successful fund-raiser and ODW raises anywhere from $500 to $1,000 with this event.

DANCES AND TALENT SHOWS

Dances

Dances are another popular annual fund-raiser. Students generally link the dance to a holiday, season, or event. Valentine's Day, St Patrick's Day, and Halloween have all been nominated over the years. Spring dances and a dance following the last day of the high-stakes MCAS (Massachusetts Comprehensive Assessment System) tests have also been proposed. Once the theme and time are voted upon, students negotiate with the administration.

First, two veterans are selected to schedule a meeting with the principal to determine if a dance is feasible and determine a date. Once the date has been set the students decide upon an admission fee and form committees such as publicity, food, setup and cleanup, finding a DJ, etc. At the weekly meetings committee members report on their progress and frustrations and engage in group problem solving. They then reconvene in groups. This process is ongoing until the actual event.

Talent Shows

In 2011, a group of students suggested a school-wide talent show as a possible fund-raising event. After considerable discussion and debate and a meeting with the principal, the students developed a plan that has evolved as a model for the event, which is held in an afternoon in May, after school. The definition of talent is broad. There are 15 acts that have included song, dance, instrumental musical performances, drama, and stand-up comedy. One year a student demonstrated how to assemble a Chinese musical instrument. During intermission, ODW students present a PowerPoint that explains the origins and purpose of ODW and describes the project that the students are currently funding.

Five prizes, plastic trophies with gold stars, are awarded. To ensure fairness, none of the judges can be middle school students or friends or family of the participants. Impartial high school students and adult volunteers are recruited to serve as judges. ODW alumni often volunteer as judges. Occasionally alumni participate as performers as well.

ODW students form committees and run the entire event. To ensure that all runs smoothly, there is a mandatory rehearsal prior to the performance. The students charge $1.00 for admission to the show. Performers pay $2.00 entry fee in order to perform their acts. There is no food allowed, but the students sell water bottles to obtain additional funds. Parents as well as students attend and ODW raises $150 to $200 from this annual event.

ONE-TIME FUND-RAISERS

An Online Celebrity Auction

Generally fund-raising ideas come from the ODW students; however, the idea for a celebrity online auction came from school's new principal Dan Gilbert's family. When Gilbert became principal of Broad Meadows Middle School he started attending ODW meetings. At his family Thanksgiving gathering he shared the story of ODW. His brother Chris Gilbert, an actor, brought his fiancé, Lesley-Ann Brandt, star of the film *Zombie Apocalypse*, to the festivities. Brandt, an actor and an activist, wanted to help by adding her name as a celebrity to the effort. She offered to donate autographed items, photographs, scripts, and other memorabilia, which the students could auction off.

In the spirit of ODW, Principal Gilbert brought this offer to the ODW meeting and asked the students if they were interested. They were VERY interested, as *Zombie Apocalypse* holds a special place in the hearts of middle school students. Fifteen ODW met with the principal after school in the computer lab to research online auction sites. They evaluated eleven auction sites. They applied the analytic skills they had learned from assessing proposals and checked the sites' ratings on the web through the charity navigator and the better business bureau sites.

The students' first choice was winning cause.org. They decided to call the Minnesota-based organization to ensure that the bulk of the proceeds would go to the ODW project. The owner of the website happened to answer the phone and graciously participated in an hour-long, after school conference call, with fifteen students, their teacher, and the principal. He provided them with advice on how to run an online auction and answered the students' questions about the benefits of his site.

The students launched the 30-day online auction on June 12, International Child Labor Day. Lesley-Ann Brandt and her fiancée, Chris Gilbert, attended the ODW meeting before the auction launch. The middle school students were thrilled.

RESPONDING TO NATIONAL AND INTERNATIONAL CRISIS

During times of crisis, the ODW community employed the skills and practices it had developed to design campaigns in response to national and international events that strongly affected them. On the home front, the students were shaken by the 9/11 bombing of the World Trade Center and Pentagon in 2001 and the Boston Marathon bombing on April 15, 2013. The students were also moved to take additional actions by the 2010 earthquake that devastated Haiti.

9/11

The Friday after 9/11, the students placed the following question at the center of their agenda: What can we do to help the children who were orphaned by 9/11? They began by researching various relief organizations and found the Twin Towers Orphans Fund.

After checking on its credibility through the office of their local Congressman, William Delahunt, the majority of ODW members voted to partner with that charity. The goal was to raise a thousand dollars by organizing a yard sale and auction, "The Red, White and Blue Auction," at Broad Meadows.

The students received the endorsement and help from the principal, Parent/Teacher's Organization, and their advisor Mr. Adams for the event. They asked teachers, parents, and local businesses to help get items for the auction and for the yard sale. According to Ron Adams:

A remarkable outpouring of donated items started arriving at Broad Meadows Middle School for the auction/yard sale. Items included signed items from the Red Sox, Bruins, Celtics, Patriots, Revolution, Breakers (women's pro soccer) as well as restaurant gift cards and hundreds of items for the yard sale, most of the items still had tags on them.

In keeping with the spirit of ODW, the students decided to include an education component. They invited local officials such as police, firefighters, military, and first responders such as doctors, nurses, and EMTs to come to the Yard Sale to speak about 9/11. Students divided up a list and tried to get spokespeople from various organizations to come to the yard sale and speak. Local flight attendants from United and American Airlines who were friends with the crews from the hijacked airplanes heard about the event and contacted the school to volunteer as speakers.

Ron described the event as "a day of healing and action." He said there was not "a dry eye at the Yard Sale/auction as the flight attendants eulogized their fallen co-workers." The students presented each speaker with a certificate of thanks and mourning. The yard sale and auction raised $3,644 for children who lost parents in the attack. This included scholarships, housing, and counseling.

The Haitian Earthquake

When the earthquake struck Haiti on January 12, 2010, the ODW veterans were already familiar with the problems Haiti faced. During the previous year they had worked to fund a Partners in Health initiative to help children and their families in Haiti. The night of the earthquake they received the following e-mail from their former partner.

Dear Friends,

A major earthquake centered just 10 miles from Port-au-Prince has devastated sections of the city and knocked out telephone communications throughout the country. Reached via e-mail, Partners in Health staff at our facilities in the Central Plateau report that they experienced a strong shock but no major damage or injuries.

In an urgent e-mail from Port-au-Prince, Louise Ivers, our clinical director in Haiti, appealed for assistance from her colleagues in the Central Plateau: "Port-au-Prince is devastated, lot of deaths. SOS. SOS. ... Temporary field hospital by us needs supplies, pain meds, and bandages. Please help us."

The earthquake has destroyed much of the already fragile and overburdened infrastructure in the most densely populated part of the country. A massive and immediate international response is needed to provide food, water, shelter, and medical supplies for tens of thousands of people.

With our hospitals and our highly trained medical staff in Haiti, Partners in Health is already mobilizing resources and preparing plans to bring medical assistance and supplies to areas that have been hardest hit. Both our teams in Boston and Haiti are already mobilizing to deliver resources as quickly as possible to the places where they are most needed.

> Thank you for your solidarity during this crisis.
> Ophelia Dahl (co-founder along with Dr. Paul Farmer)
> Executive Director

Broad Meadows ODW called an emergency meeting in response to the crisis. The students voted to put their fund-raising for the year's project on hold and spent the next month working to raise money to help earthquake victims in Haiti. They decided to evenly divide the proceeds between two nonprofits, Partners in Health and the St. Boniface Haiti Foundation, and launched the Hearts for Haiti campaign.

In keeping with what they had learned about the School for Iqbal Campaign, the students decided to select a symbolic donation number. The $12.00 donation request represented Iqbal's age at the time of his death and the amount of his family's initial debt to the carpet manufacturer. The Haitian earthquake measured 7.0 on the Richter scale and the students decided to e-mail the schools across the state and ask for contributions of $7.00. Individual students raised money at local churches and sporting events. At Broad Meadows, they publicized the crisis and placed a collection container in the cafeteria. They collected over $400.00.

For their final effort the students decided to organize a raffle for Haiti. They formed committees and contacted local businesses, sporting venues, and celebrities and asked for donations for the raffle. They wanted to combine an educational component with the raffle and decided on a school-wide assembly in which guest speakers would precede the raffle. The school administration granted the ODW students' request and a relief worker from one of the partner organizations, the St. Boniface Haitian Foundation, addressed the entire Broad Meadows student body at a special assembly dedicated to earthquake relief.

As a result of their efforts, within the span of a month, the ODW students raised $3,000 and awareness of the plight of the Haitian earthquake victims throughout the community and the state of Massachusetts!

Boston Marathon Bombing

When the Boston Marathon attacks occurred on April 15, 2015, the students decided to add a second project to aid the victims. They researched aid organizations and they chose the One Fund Boston as a partner. The students wanted to be sure that every victim was remembered and given help and felt that the One Fund Boston would accomplish this goal. The students collected gift cards from local restaurants and held a Boston Strong drawing and raised over $1,000.

As time went on the students learned about the newly established Martin Richard Charitable Foundation. The foundation was formed by parents of Martin Richard, the 8-year-old boy who was killed by the bomb blast at the marathon finish line and is known as the MR8 fund. Each year marathon participants volunteer to raise funds for the MR8 foundation through collecting pledges. The foundation then invests in education, athletics, and community in the Boston area in Martin's memory. It has become a tradition that ODW Broad Meadows will remember 8-year-old Martin by participating in a modest fund-raiser each school year.

The students decided to further honor the memory of the Boston Marathon bombing victims by adding a blue and yellow ribbon, the colors of the Boston Marathon, to the sleeve of the ODW T-shirt.

EDUCATION FOR GLOBAL AWARENESS

Partner Organizations

The year-long relationship with the partner NGO has become a key mechanism for educating students about the issues faced by youth in the developing world. New technologies allow for real-time connections with both agency representatives and youth overseas. This personal contact makes the issues and the campaign more personal and relevant for the students in ODW.

Once the voting has been completed, the students engage in an "ODW ritual," notifying the winning grant applicant. The students gather in Ron's classroom, room 109, and Ron puts his cell on speakerphone. All of the students gather around and some of the veteran ODW students get the honor of telling the director of the organization that the votes have been counted and their organization was selected. The response on the other end is often emotional. Several of the partners have cried on receiving the news of the additional funding.

The students then ask the partner organization what they can do together to inform the school community and the wider community about what is going on. They ask for their partner's assistance in spreading the word and raising funds. Through the partnership and technology, they are able to learn about the detail of the daily lives of the youth in the villages they are supporting and the strategies the partner organization is using to assist in creating change. The ongoing relationship with the partner organization provides them with the opportunity to ask questions throughout the school year. ODW's relationship with Goodweave illustrates this educational model.

Goodweave

Goodweave was founded in 1995 by 2014 Nobel Prize laureate Kailash Satyarthi. As the chair of the South Asian Coalition on Child Servitude, he was involved in rescuing child laborers and returning them to their homes. After one of these raids, he was at the train station returning home when he saw dozens of children on the platform with a middleman headed for the looms. He realized that no matter how many children he rescued, there would be a limitless supply to replace them. Satyarthi had an epiphany, the best way to end child labor in the carpet industry would be through raising consumer awareness and creating a mechanism for corporate accountability, a radical concept in the mid-1990s. From this idea, Goodweave, originally called Rugmark, was born (Goodweave, 2016).

According to Goodweave Executive Director Nina Smith, Goodweave's aim was to cultivate consumer demand for child labor-free carpets, develop a rigorous certification system that insured that no child laborers are used in carpet production, and get businesses to buy into the concept. Developing the system took many years. When Goodweave was launched it was not common for activists and businesses to work together and Goodweave became a pioneer in this area. Smith said:

> Initially, businesses were scared and none of the companies would talk to us. We started with the rug buying community and got a couple of high end carpet designers, like Stephanie Odegard and John Kurtz of New Moon to sign on and do promotions. It moved slowly. It took fifteen years for the movement to blossom. We've signed Macy's and Restoration Hardware and Target. All the things that needed to be aligned are now in place. Goodweave products are now available at every price point and design on the market ...

Goodweave currently monitors manufacturers in India, Nepal, and Afghanistan whose products are marketed in the United States, the United Kingdom, and Germany. Importers who join Goodweave must commit to employing workers at or above the legal working age; 18 in India, 14 in Nepal, and 15 in Afghanistan. These importers must agree to open all weaving facilities for unannounced, random inspection checks. If they pass inspection, they are issued certification labels for their rugs that guarantee that their products are child labor free.

The licensed importers are charged a fee for the Goodweave labels, based upon the shipment values of the carpets. The majority of the funds derived from these fees are used to help former child laborers and finance Goodweave

marketing campaigns. Children rescued during inspection checks are provided with a temporary home, counseling, and medical treatment and are
brought back to their families. Once family reunification has occurred, Goodweave fully sponsors the child's education till the 10th grade. The children
first receive intensive training in literacy and math and then move on to formal
education that includes science, social studies, language, mathematics, and
extracurricular activities such as music and art.

In addition to its rescue and rehabilitation work, Goodweave works to
promote the well-being of workers in the weaving community and prevent
child labor. They provide day care, early childhood education, and school
sponsorship for the children of adult weavers. They also provide the community with adult literacy classes and health clinics. Since its inception,
Goodweave has rescued and provided services for over 3,600 former child
laborers and sponsored the education of 12,500 children in the weaving
community.

UNICEF and the US Department of Labor have verified that the number
of children employed in the carpet industry in India, Nepal, and Afghanistan
has dropped from over a million to 250,000 since Goodweave began its work.
The organization is looking to expand its work in the carpet weaving industry
to China and Pakistan. In addition, they are attempting to apply their strategy
for eliminating child labor to the brick industry. Two years ago, Goodweave
partnered with Humanity United and Global Fairness to introduce "Better
Brick" to Nepal where 175,000 children work in the kilns.

ODW Partnerships with Goodweave

ODW first partnered with Goodweave in the 2011–2012 school year. The
students voted to fund a proposal to assist 40 rescued child laborers from the
Nepali rug weaving industry. The money would be used to provide counseling, room and board, and health care for the children. It would also pay for
their education for a year.

By partnering with Goodweave, the middle school students saw that ethical
consumer practice could affect change. They learned about the workings of
the organization and the plight of child laborers in Nepal through face-to-face
contact with Goodweave's Executive Director Nina Smith who traveled from
Washington, DC to attend an after school meeting at Broad Meadows and
educate and support the ODW students.

Smith, a native of Glen Falls, New York, studied International Relations
at Tufts University. Before coming to Goodweave in 1999, she worked
as Executive Director of the Crafts Center, a nonprofit that assists indigenous grassroots artisans with technical and market access. She also served

as a crafts consultant to the Tibetan government in exile in India and was a founder of the Fair Trade Federation in Washington, DC. She has headed Goodweave for 16 years.

The granddaughter of Holocaust survivors, Smith feels that her interest in social justice stems from her early family encounters. She said:

> I remember going to meet my cousin, Mark. He was eight when he went to Auschwitz. He told us about surviving a concentration camp … the pits of dead bodies. He had a number tattooed on his arm. My grandmother was a very socially active woman and it had an influence on me.
>
> When I first learned about child labor, I felt that there were parallels. The story about what was happening to the Jews was out there, but there weren't enough people picking up on it and taking action. I wanted to be one of the people who heard the story of child labor and found outlets for action.

Nina was first moved to take action by the story of Iqbal. She read an interview with him in Vanity Fair and decided that child labor was something she really wanted to work on. She knew about Ron Adams, the School for Iqbal Campaign, and ODW and was pleased when Goodweave received a phone call from an ODW member asking the organization to submit a proposal.

On Nina Smith's first visit to ODW, Nina proposed a fund-raising idea. She asked the students if they would be interested raffling a Goodweave rug, valued at several thousand dollars, if she could convince a manufacturer to donate a rug. The students embraced the idea and all of the ODW schools voted to participate in the rug raffle. The raffle provided the students with a mechanism to educate the public about child labor. Ron Adams said:

> Raffle tickets were distributed to every member school. The raffle brought the idea of consumer responsibility right to the forefront. Consumers make decisions every day about whether they are going to shop for the best price, look for something that is ethically made or not think about it at all. The raffle brought this home.

Toward the end of the school year, Nina Smith arranged for the Broad Meadows students to communicate with the Nepali students they had sponsored on Skype. The online face-to-face contact made the partnership more meaningful for all involved. Ron said, "The students can't travel, but technology helps to bridge geographical distances."

ODW voted to partner with Goodweave again in 2013–2014. They worked to fund education for 250 young girls in three villages in India's Uttar Pradesh province, many of whom had no previous schooling.

Student-Initiated Education for Empathy Programs

ODW encourages students to design its activist agenda. In addition to education and fund-raising programs, students have developed and enacted programs designed to self-educate through building empathy and understanding.
Two of the most unusual student-initiated programs are Krista's Challenge
and Day of the Goats—Hands on Empathy.

Krista's Challenge

During the first ODW/Goodweave campaign to assist Nepalese children,
8th grader Krista began to realize how much American youth take luxury
technology items for granted. She learned from a classmate from Nepal that
students in some parts of Nepal don't even have running water and that daily
survival can be a luxury.

Krista proposed that ODW sponsor a "technology fast" wherein students
and teachers pledge to give up technology for 24 hours and use their time
away from luxury items to think about the plight of Nepalese children. After
voting and debate, the students selected 3:00 pm, Monday, March 28, 2011
to 3:00 pm, Tuesday, March 29, 2011 as the fast date. The students spread
news of the action through posters in the school cafeteria and flyers that
they delivered to classrooms. In addition to fasting, they asked for $12.00
contributions (the price of Iqbal's bond), to ODW's Goodweave campaign to
support rescued child laborers in Nepal. The local Quincy paper, The Patriot
Ledger, picked up on the story and their publicity added to the "technology
fast's" momentum.

Day of the Goats—Hands on Empathy

ODW partnered with the American Foundation for Children with AIDS
(AFCAIDS), two times: in 2011–2012 and again in 2014–2015. The goal
of the 2011–2012 project was to provide seeds, high nutrient daily por-
ridge, health care, and livestock and livestock training to AIDS orphans in
Zimbabwe whose parents had perished as a result of the AIDS epidemic and
now lived in orphan-run households. The resources and training promote
self-reliance and the resources to sustain their families. In 2014–2015, the
project's goal was the same; however, 80% of the aid was sent to families
in Zimbabwe and the remaining 20% was sent to families in similar straits
in Uganda.

During the spring of 2015, 6th grader Abigail Drinkwater came up with
an idea for building empathy. She was a member of the Massachusetts
4-H club and volunteered at Weir River farm, a 75-acre working farm

in Hingham, Massachusetts. Based upon her farming experiences, she believed that her ODW classmates could develop a better understanding of the challenges faced by their peers in Zimbabwe and Uganda if they spent a day doing farmwork with chickens and goats. She offered to try to arrange a day for the students to come to Weir River Farm to work with the chickens and goats.

Abigail met with the director of the farm and they drew up a program for the ODW volunteers. Twelve students signed up and along with Ron Adams and a parent chaperone, they spent the day shoveling poop, changing the straw in the barn, and working with livestock. In the process they learned first-hand how difficult it is to farm and be a farmer and gained a deeper understanding of the daily lives of the Zimbabwe orphans.

ANNUAL YEAR-END EVENTS

The Day's Work

Every year ODW students complete a day of work to raise money for their partner project. Students at the Broad Meadows chapter do volunteer work in their local community to find local sponsors for their work who pledge donations for the annual project. In this way two communities are helped—Quincy and the community overseas.

Students are encouraged to design their own workdays. Over the years they have chosen to volunteer at the local senior center where they served food, helped clean up, and played cards with the residents; clean the city's naval museum; clean the local animal shelter; and assist with the letter carrier food drive by helping to sort and unload donations at the local food pantry. In addition to the individually designed projects, each year the group works to "beautify" the grounds of the Thomas Crane Public Library by clearing and planting flowers in the garden outside the Children's Room. The garden has been dubbed the Iqbal Masih Children's Peace Garden. The planting of the garden has become an annual ODW ritual and as with all rituals it has developed its own symbols.

The origins of the garden predate ODW. Shortly after Iqbal's death on April 16, 1995, the students planted a miniature weeping cherry tree in the garden outside the children's room of the library. In an e-mail to ODW students Ron told the students:

> The tree reminded us of Iqbal ... dwarfed by child labor, malnutrition and abuse ... bent over. ... The tree blooms every year. ... It's as if Iqbal's dream of freedom and education for all children comes alive every year on April 16th. (e-mail, April 16, 2013)

In addition to the tree, the students plant flowers each year. Pansies, of all colors and sizes, are the flowers of choice, Ron said, "because they look like children and it seems like the children of the world are looking back at you."

Like other ODW events, gardening work day takes considerable work and organization. Students need to go to local businesses that sell flowers and ask for donations of flowers and mulch. Ron provides an official letter on the ODW letterhead that includes its logo, website information, and e-mail address. The following letter from 2009 is typical of the kind of correspondence that goes out to the Quincy community.

Dear Flower Seller,

I am a student who is *volunteering this week to plant flowers at the Thomas Crane Public Library* in Quincy Center, but I do not have flowers to plant. *Could you donate flowering plants for this cause?*

This is the ninth year my school has beautified the library, but it's my first time being part of the project.

The club I belong to at my school is called "Operation Day's Work." It has won many awards. The goal of the club is to help improve TWO communities with ONE day's work.

Locally—we will plant flowers at our library.

Globally—people sponsor our flower planting. We donate 100% of the pledges to building a school, health clinic or orphanage in a developing country. For the last TEN years, my school has successfully worked with 13 other US schools to work ONE day and fund a school, health clinic or orphanage in Haiti, El Salvador, Nepal, Bangladesh, Vietnam, Rwanda, Burundi, Ethiopia and Haiti again this year. *Details are on our website.*

Please help both communities by donating flowers which we can plant at the Thomas Crane Library in Quincy Center.

It is amazing what youth can do in a day!

On the Saturday planting day, students and chaperones arrive at 9:00. Mrs. Claire Fitzmaurice, the President of the local garden club, instructs the students on the art of flower planting. Typically, turnout is high, ranging from 25 to 45, in a given year. Volunteers include both current ODW students and alumni who return to partake in the annual event.

The T-Shirt Ceremony

Each year the students gather for the final ODW meeting where they receive an official ODW T-shirt as a reward and memento of the year's work. The shirts are white cotton and have the ODW logo printed on the front, and a list of projects dating from 1999 to the present is printed on the back. In keeping with the ODW philosophy, no child labor can be used to produce or manufacture the T-shirts. To ensure that the shirts are child labor free, the students researched companies and decided to use EDUN-Live to supply the T-shirts and Mirror Image, a Rhode Island union silk screening company, to do the printing. The silk screening is paid for by the Good People Fund, an award-winning philanthropic organization based in New Jersey.

EDUN-Live was founded by Ali Hewson and her husband, U2 singer Bono. The company promotes sustainable development in Africa and provides training and development for adults in cotton production, sewing, and other skills necessary to make a living in the textile industry. The ODW USA leaders submit a letter to EDUN requesting the donation of blank tees. EDUN has donated 72 blank tees for the past 6 years. The tees are shipped from Ireland to Mirror Image, which is owned by Rick Roth, the coordinator of the Somerville Amnesty International chapter. Roth has been involved with the group since the School for Iqbal days, when he helped the students develop their first website.

Roth renews his commitment to ODW each year by printing the T-shirts and attending the annual ceremony. In May 2009 Roth arrived at room 109 with two large cardboxes filled with T-shirts. Ron Adams began the ceremony on a somber note. He held up a pencil drawing of Iqbal Masih by an artist in California, entitled Unfinished Prayer. He said:

In 1994, Iqbal came to our school. He told his story and asked for help. He opened our eyes. He asked for things that we take for granted … like education. Let's have a moment of silence in Iqbal's memory.

He then continued:

These T-shirts were donated by Ali Hewson, Bono's wife. They are child labor free. No one was hurt making these shirts. The environment was not hurt making these shirts.

Ron introduces Rick Roth and tells the students about his connection with Amnesty International, Iqbal, and The Kid's Campaign and his annual contribution of printing the ODW T-shirts. He then says to the students:

This year 2,000 students in Haiti will go to school because of your work. You should be very proud. I want you to nominate someone to get a shirt and explain why.

Ron, then models the process with one of the 8th-grade girls. He calls her name and says I nominate you because of your dedication and activism. She comes to the front of the room and receives a T-shirt. The students applaud. She nominates the next student and says, "I nominate you because you have been active in ODW for many years." The affirmations continue:

You developed the courage to come up and talk.
You were always so devoted.
You work hard and are always here.
You try your best, no matter where you are.
You are always willing to help out in any way.

The affirmations and applause continue. Then the group poses for pictures in their T-shirts. Ron says:

> There are lots of ways to raise awareness. I hope that you will use these shirts to tell the story. There are lots of good people behind these shirts. It's rare to meet a group of kids as good as you. You are all stars all the way.

He wishes the veterans well on their journey to high school and tells the 6th and 7th graders to rest up over the summer and come back prepared to change the world. The veterans linger chatting with each other and waiting to say goodbye to their favorite teacher mentor.

CONCLUSION

During the second half of the school year the ODW community builds upon the shared knowledge and practices developed during the first half of the year. Rituals that have become a part of the groups' repertoire are reenacted and shared with the "newbies." While planning for the hot cocoa sale, Penny Power, the annual dance, the talent show, and most importantly the day's work, the newbies hear stories about these events. By participating in their organization and enactment, they share in this history and solidify their identity with the group.

While traditions are important for the group to reproduce itself, innovation is a key element of the community. Krista's Challenge and the Day of the Goat illustrate the students' practice of 21st-century skills such as critical thinking, agility, and the willingness to take risks and try new ventures. However, the vibrancy of the community is best illustrated by students' impromptu responses to national and international crises.

In response to 9/11, the earthquake in Haiti, and the Boston Marathon bombing, the students called emergency meetings, researched organizations, and developed action plans. They functioned as a democratic entity, voted on a project, formed committees, and developed fund-raising and educational events. The actions of three distinct groups of participants at different points in the history of ODW demonstrate that participants internalized the skills and practices of the community and were able to transfer them to new situations.

Throughout the second half of the school year the ODW community is continuously "taking action" to improve conditions in the global community. Through working with their partner organizations, not only do they investigate the world beyond their immediate environment, but they are exposed to "globally competent adults" who have dedicated their lives to improving the world and who serve as powerful role models.

The story of Iqbal, the injustice of child labor, and the importance of being a responsible consumer are repeated throughout the year in a variety of contexts. Students were exposed to the ignorance and/or indifference of store managers in Child Labor-Free Shopping Trip. However, they encounter fair trade cocoa venders, carpets vetted by Goodweave, and T-shirts produced and screened without exploiting children. In the final T-shirt ceremony, the newbies symbolically become full participants; old timers are ready to inaugurate next year's group.

Chapter 8

Portraits of ODW Activists

I don't know if I would have gone to college if I hadn't joined ODW.

—Mike

MIKE'S STORY

Ron Adams and ODW provided Mike with a path to develop competence and confidence in his academic abilities. Mike was a popular student athlete at Broad Meadows. In 6th and 7th grade he was in the "extra help" classes and was not allowed to participate in the regular classes. He said:

> When it came to reading and writing, I didn't have the opportunity to have Mr. Adams as a teacher. And he did these assignments—I remember one of them was going to interview people who had lived in the WWII era with a tape recorder and to write down your report. I did it on my own, because I wanted to do it so badly, and I just passed it in to my teacher, Mrs. Todd. She was shocked that I just went out and did it and I guess she passed it on to Mr. Adams.
>
> One day he pulled me aside and just told me how good of a job I did and how proud of me he was. It meant a lot to me because I wanted to be in the regular writing class so bad. There was another instance when I wrote a short story, and somehow again he got a hold of it and he went out of his way to tell me how good it was. It meant so much that I wanted to join ODW to show that I was as smart as the other kids. I could do well too. That was my main reason, I wanted to impress him ... and there were a lot of good looking girls.

Mike felt that Mr. Adams really went out of his way to make new students feel welcome. As an icebreaker for newcomers, he would introduce the

student to the entire group and then have each member introduce her/himself.
He'd follow by jokingly saying, "Why do you want to join? You have to be
here on Fridays!" Mike said:

> For me, it was like a large dose of Iqbal in a small amount of time. ... It was like
> overnight, I grew so passionate about it. It was always the idea of helping out a
> child who didn't have a chance like I did.
>
> All the stories and the newspaper articles hanging up in Mr. Adams class-
> room, just watching my fellow students in action was unbelievable. He had this
> way of finding leaders and I guess he saw leadership in me because I was an
> athlete, and I brought a different kind of leadership to the program. I think he
> wanted me to be involved. He found ways to keep me inspired.

In addition to attending the Constitutional Convention in Philadelphia
and the follow-up conference the next summer in Minnesota, Mike represented the group on numerous speaking engagements. The ODW presentation at Harvard University Graduate School of Education was among
the most memorable. The Broad Meadows students addressed graduate
students and professors. Mike said that as a middle school student he found
the experience unbelievable. He still has a piece of chalk that he kept as a
souvenir.

The 8th-grade awards ceremony was another pivotal experience for Mike.
He didn't have high honors but Ron asked him to come and work backstage.
It was a trick. Mike and Beth received the American Legion Award for their
work in ODW. Mike had to come from backstage to accept the award. His
parents had been informed of the surprise and they were at the ceremony.
Mike remembers feeling very happy. He said, "Broad Meadows really knows
how to help out kids. I'm glad that I went there."

Mike continued his work with ODW through the 10th grade. In 2001, after
9/11, he worked on the yard sale fund-raiser. Mike was in charge of publicity.
He got his friends involved and they went around Quincy, hanging up flyers
and talking to people.

Family Background

Mike is Quincy born and bred. His parents supported his work in ODW. They
wanted him to be involved in after school activities and encouraged him to try
things. They felt that involvement would keep him out of trouble.

Mike's father is a printer. He has been working at a printing press his entire
life. While Mike feels that printing is a dying trade, he says that his father is
still working because he works hard and knows how to run the big printing
presses on his own.

As a child, Mike wanted to enter into his father's trade. One night his father woke him up in the middle of the night and said, "Whatever you do Michael, don't be a printer. Go to college." His father's words resonated with him and made him want to do better in school.

When he was a child, Mike's mother worked as a waitress at the Sheraton Towers in Boston. She met Jim Rice, the Red Sox player, when she was working there. There was a table that ran up a $500.00 tab, but the customers left no tip. She was pregnant with Mike and she started to cry. Jim Rice saw her crying and bought her a huge sundae. Then he left her a $200 tip.

That story made a big impression on Mike.

When his mom left the Sheraton, she was given the opportunity to run the Germantown Community Center at St. Boniface Church in the Germantown Housing Projects in Quincy. The job paid poorly, about $15,000 a year, and there was no working computer. However, she was able to develop a thriving center with programs that still exist today. These include a food pantry and a program to feed more than a thousand Quincy families on Thanksgiving and Christmas; a "Dress for Success" program for adult females going on job interviews, and leadership training programs for youth. Mike worked at the center all through high school and still helps out by running groups. He is really proud of what his mom has achieved and calls the center a "great place."

Education and Career

Mike attended St. Joseph's College in Maine. He majored in history and minored in secondary education. When he returned to Quincy, he couldn't find a job. So he waited tables and worked for his mother at the Germantown Community Center. He finally got a full-time job as a substitute Social Studies teacher at Quincy High School. He loved the job but it only lasted for eight months. His subbing stint was followed by job teaching in a behavioral autism class which he described as the best teaching experience he ever had because "once you teach there, you can do anything, and I mean anything."

He next took a job as assistant manager at Training Resources in Quincy, an agency that runs education programs for low-income, out-of-school young adults between the ages of 14 and 24. These include Young Parents, an English as a Second Language (ESL), General Education Diploma (GED), and parenting training program for pregnant and parenting teens; Achieve Youth Opportunity Program, a GED, vocational training, and job assistance program for out-of-school youth; and Youth Build, a GED, onsite construction training, and job placement assistance program.

Youth Build is Mike's favorite of the three. He really likes the combination of GED and job training. In Quincy they build houses for veterans of Iraq and Afghanistan wars. They are paid $8.00 an hour and work 25 hours per week.

The houses are built from scratch and Mike feels that the participants in the Youth Build do a really nice job. He believes that the program makes a real difference in their lives.

Impact of ODW

Mike entered an employee leadership training program and was promoted. He now manages the Worchester office of Training Resources of America. He attributes his sense of agency and civic efficacy to his work at the German-town Community Center and to ODW. He felt that as a participant in ODW he acquired leadership skills and learned about the value of hard work, a bit about the world, and how government works. He also became more skilled at public speaking and he feels really comfortable speaking in front of a crowd.

Mike defines citizenship in terms of helping others. He feels that good citizens are people like Ron and his mother who did a lot to help people all of the time. While ODW made Mike aware of problems worldwide, he said that his current focus is local and national. He feels that in his current position he is developing the same types of youth education programs in Massachusetts that ODW sought to fund overseas.

ODW provided Mike with the impetus he needed to push ahead academi-cally and go on to college. For him it was a game changer. He said:

> I really wouldn't have gone to college without Ron and the program. ... It made me a better student. It made me care about school. All of the students that were involved were the smartest students, who did really well, got all of the awards and were always recognized. I worked my hardest, but I just never got there. ODW made me work harder. I was inspired by my own classmates.

Rita

> When I told my mom that we were doing a project to help girls in Vietnam, she said, "If I had stayed in Vietnam that might have been you."—Rita

Background

Rita is a first-generation American. She grew up in Quincy where she still resides. Her mother is from Vietnam and her father is from Taiwan. Her parents met in the United States. Rita's mother worked as a teacher's aide at a preschool. Her father was a salesman at a bakery. The family emphasized education and Rita was raised very strictly. The routine was school, library, home. Rita said:

> Education is a really big value in my family. My parents were very supportive of anything that is related to education. If I needed to go to the library they

pushed for it. At the elementary school I went to there was a summer program that my parents tried to get me to participate in every year. I ended up falling in love with the program and I volunteered there as a teacher's aide for quite a number of years.

Rita first learned about ODW in 7th grade when she had Mr. Adams for Language Arts. He showed her class a video about Iqbal and the School for Iqbal Campaign. She was inspired by the story and wanted to become a part of ODW. However, her parents wouldn't let her stay after school for meetings. She spoke with Mr. Adams about her dilemma and he suggested that she write thank you notes for the donations that were still coming in for the school in Pakistan. She could write the thank you notes at home and contribute in that way. In 8th grade, her parents granted her more freedom and she was allowed to participate in after school activities that met her parents' approval. She became active in ODW that year.

While community service was not stressed at home, Rita engaged her parents' sympathies by telling them the story of Iqbal. However, the impetus to get involved came from Rita. She was drawn to ODW because she felt she was helping two communities: youth in developing countries and the local community of Quincy. She inspired her younger sister who also became involved. Her experience at Broad Meadows inspired her to develop an ODW chapter at North Quincy High School. She didn't realize until much later that her parents were proud of her activism. She overheard her father telling her uncle in Taiwan about what she had accomplished and he said, "This is where she did most of her growing up."

ODW at North Quincy High School

Rita entered North Quincy High School in September 2001. She wanted to bring ODW to North Quincy. She said it was an opportunity to "grow ODW as well as bring something familiar with me from middle school to high school." However, she was shy and didn't know how to proceed. She went to her Dean. He volunteered to serve as advisor, if she would recruit students.

Then 9/11 struck and students were angry and wanted to do something. Mr. Adams called a meeting at the Quincy Public Library for students who were currently involved with ODW Broad Meadows and ODW alumni at local high schools: North Quincy High School, Quincy High School, and Archbishop Williams. The students decided to develop a city-wide yard sale to raise money for youth who were affected by 9/11.

Rita represented North Quincy High School at the meeting and started the North Quincy ODW chapter by recruiting students to participate in this event. She also spoke out in her English class and led an effort to write letters of condolences to families affected by the tragedy. She also arranged for ODW to become an outlet for upper division students who could get credit for community service.

During the early years North Quincy ODW was small and the majority of the active students were Rita's friends. They participated in meetings, voting, and a variety of fund-raising activities. High school was busier than middle school and there were many more extracurricular activities. Due to time constraints they organized ODW differently. While the organization was still student run, they elected student officers who took over specific functions: president, secretary, treasurer. They met twice a month instead of meeting weekly.

Voting was done differently as well. Rita would station herself in a room for two and a half hours after school and ODW members would come to pick up proposals. They would analyze the proposals and compile lists of pros and cons. Then they would go through the lists and Rita would compile them and send out the lists to all the members. Voting was done electronically and the final results were sent to the national ODW advisor.

ODW members developed their own unique fund-raising projects. They designed, hand-crafted and sold beaded animals which they called "crystal babies." They also crafted and sold customized ornaments that had an inside space to place a photograph. They developed a cleaning service for teachers. They would stay after school and clean desks and teachers would donate between $8.00 and $10.00 for this service.

Rita worked hard to develop North Quincy ODW. By the time she graduated membership had grown from five to over forty students. Rita's sister took over when she left and worked to maintain an active chapter.

Rita moved on to the University of Massachusetts at Dartmouth. She feels that her experience with ODW influenced her choice of major and career. She said:

> I really enjoyed helping people and I saw ODW as a great outlet to do so. I was really into community service and that being the case, I wanted my career to be in community service or at least serving others in some capacity.

Rita studied psychology and business at college. She interned at a nonprofit where she honed the skills and lessons she had learned from ODW: public speaking, fund-raising, event planning, time management, and the value of writing thank you letters. At the nonprofit she learned about grant writing and correspondence. Upon graduation Rita looked for work at a nonprofit but because of the economy she was not able to find work in this area. She works at an accounting firm in learning and development and feels that she is gaining experience in coaching and developing others. She wants to go to graduate school and sees herself as "an eternal student of sorts."

Rita still volunteers. She works on the side for a nonprofit doing data management cleanup. She has also prepared income taxes for low-income people and/or students who cannot afford someone to prepare their taxes. Her consumer habits have also been influenced by her participation in ODW. She never has nor will ever purchase Nike products. She tries to avoid Wal-Mart and only shops at stores that treat workers fairly and purchases products that have been made fairly. She said:

> ODW was a great opportunity to think more globally; especially with child labor laws. ... It gives young people the chance to think about world affairs. I think that given there is so much testing involved in education and it is so much more about the bottom line, I feel that ODW is a great way for students to get outside their comfort zone and learn and be exposed to things that they wouldn't be exposed to in their normal education.

Mia

A good citizen is someone who will not turn a blind eye.—Mia

Mia was born in Bangkok, Thailand, and came to the United States when she was just 2 years old. Her mother is Chinese and her father is Vietnamese. They both left their countries and moved to Thailand and then fled Thailand because of the war. Her family chose to come to Boston because there was a Vietnamese community and network that helped people to get settled and find jobs. Her dad worked as a machinist and her mom worked as a babysitter.

Mia is one of four children. Both of her older brothers dropped out of high school and went into the trades. Her younger brother is in the restaurant business and studying at Quincy College. Mia attended Syracuse University where she studied entrepreneurship, retail, and marketing management.

In 2001, when Mia was in 7th grade, she attended an ODW student-led presentation at Broad Meadows. It was her first introduction to ODW. She said that learning about child labor and the plight of youth in other countries, "really touched me. I felt that they didn't deserve this and that I didn't deserve what I had either. I think it was the injustice ... the way my life was and the way their lives were."

Mia started going to ODW meetings. At first she was very quiet, but as she learned more, she started speaking up and her level of involvement increased. By 8th grade she was taking on leadership roles in both speaking and fund-raising. She said:

> ODW was definitely a safe space because every idea that we said out loud would be written down and no ideas were ever shot down. We all listened to one

another. ... We sort of went through the list of ideas and narrowed them down, but nobody's feeling got hurt.

We really worked together.

Activism and service were not stressed in Mia's home. Her mother was more education oriented. She used to push them to do well in school, but that was it. Mia said that at first her mother did not understand, but was pleased that Mia was doing something good. As she gained a deeper understanding of ODW, she became very supportive of Mia's work. However, the impetus to get involved came from Mia.

When Mia graduated and moved on to Quincy High School, she didn't want to quit ODW, so she decided to develop a branch there. She went to the principal and explained ODW to him. He helped her to find a meeting space and an advisor to assist with the meetings.

The ODW chapter at Quincy High used a structure similar to North Quincy High. There were elected officers and biweekly meetings. The membership voted for the annual project and engaged in fund-raising. The biggest project was an annual holiday fair fund-raiser.

Mia felt that her leadership skills grew and developed as a result of this project. As president of the fledgling ODW organization she felt over-whelmed and responsible for organizing the Holiday Fair. At first she tried to micro-manage the event and some of her closest friends pulled her aside and told her that she needed to learn to trust that they could do this. She felt that she not only learned how to organize and manage an event from this experi-ence, but also how to motivate people, develop trust, and delegate responsibil-ity. She believes that these skills have helped her in college and in her career.

At the end of Mia's sophomore year in high school, Ron contacted her and asked if she would be interested in representing the United States at the Second Children's World Congress on Child Labor and Education in New Delhi, India, in September 2005. Mia accepted and during the first week of her junior year in high school, she flew to New Delhi and served as one of two US representatives.

The conference was sponsored by the Global March against Child Labor and it brought together former child laborers and child labor activists from around the world. They spent four days from September 4th to 8th exchanging stories and developing a campaign to end child labor and provide universal education for all. When the congress ended the delegates marched for several miles in India to let everyone know the message that they were trying to send. Mia said:

> I got to meet kids from all over the world. Some were former child laborer them-selves and just hearing their stories was amazing. The people that I met stood out. They kept telling me to keep doing what I was doing and to never give up.

Mia believes that the experiences she had as a result of her participation in ODW have had a lasting impact. Although Mia majored in entrepreneurship retail and marketing management at Syracuse, she realized that many of the retail jobs her fellow students were obtaining at graduation would cause them to turn a blind eye to child labor in the production of merchandise. She knew that because of her experiences at ODW she could not go against her values and do this. She decided to work in management, but not in retail. She currently works in hospitality at the Sheraton at Copley Prudential in Boston.

ODW has also affected her behavior as a consumer. She shops fair trade and won't buy Nike. Mia considers herself a global citizen and says that a good citizen is someone who will not turn a blind eye.

A FAMILY OF ACTIVISTS

We were raised with high expectations and our parents from the beginning instilled a sense of responsibility for others—Beth B

Family Background

All seven of the B. kids, Beth, Mary, Laura, Kristen, Tom, Julie, and Caroline, have been active in ODW. The oldest sisters, Beth and Mary, participated in its founding activities. For the B. kids, ODW was a logical extension of their home.

Their mother Roberta grew up in Rhode Island. She attended Catholic School for the first eight years of her schooling and then moved to public high school. At Boston College, she studied Special Education and became a teacher of the severely handicapped. She met her husband William after college when they were both teaching at the same school. Roberta taught for 5 years. After Beth was born, she began working for the Massachusetts State Board of Education in the field of teacher licensure and certification. She has worked for the state board for over 25 years.

William is Quincy born and bred. His family lives in the same house that he grew up in. He attended the Quincy public school system and went on to Boston College. Like his wife, he studied Special Education. He worked with the moderate and severe needs populations for 14 years before becoming an assistant principal at Clifford Marshall Elementary School in Quincy. William says that growing up, he learned about the importance of doing community service from doing volunteer work at one of the local parishes in the Germantown housing projects. He said, "I used to do a lot of work with youth groups and volunteer groups and that fostered my sense of community service and made me realize how important it is to society."

Both William and Roberta promoted civic engagement and fostered a sense of civic efficacy through service with their children. Their sense of service is rooted in their Catholic upbringing. They both feel that service and social justice are essential components of the Catholic tradition. William said:

> Beth and all of my kids had a sense of community service, through my wife, who felt that community service was part of bringing up kids and she loved to see it in educational settings. That was part of the reason we initially sent the kids to Catholic school. ...We believe that we have to give back. The world is much bigger than yourself and you need to do something for others.

William and Roberta decided to move their children from Catholic School to Broad Meadows because there were more community service programs there. In 7th grade there was a mandatory local community service project where students needed to do something tangible at the local level. The students started a local recycling project and did fund-raising drives for the local homeless shelters.

In addition to school projects, Roberta had her children develop neighborhood community service initiatives. They were involved in coat drives or food drives before they went to Broad Meadows. William said:

> They had the strong influence of the Catholic tradition at home; it was modelled for them. Then getting to a place like Broad Meadows where it was part of the curriculum and bumping into a guy like Ron Adams ... that is where it took off ... Ron has this amazing passion ... he brings out the best in kids and tells them they can do amazing things. He empowers kids ... its infectious!!

Beth: Middle School Activism

Beth is the oldest child. She transferred from Catholic school to Broad Meadows when she was in 7th grade. It was the last year of The Kid's Campaign. She remembered when she first heard of about A School for Iqbal:

> I heard an announcement. Mr. Adams was my homeroom teacher and I asked him about it. He said, "Come to a meeting." And I loved it right from the get go. At this point they had just built the school, so I got to hear about that. Mr. Adams had them brief me on the campaign and speak about why they personally got involved. Mr. Adams also had videos and footages of Iqbal. Seeing him and hearing it firsthand had an impact.

Beth attended several more meetings. Then Dr. David Parker visited Broad Meadows. Dr. Parker is an occupational health physician and epidemiologist at the Park Nicollet Clinic in Minneapolis. In 1992, Parker began photographing child laborers around the world. He has photographed working children in the United States, Guatemala, Ecuador, Peru, Bolivia, Sierra Leone, Mexico,

Thailand, Nepal, India, and Bangladesh. His photographs have been exhibited around the world and he has published three books: *Before Their Time: The World of Child Labor* (2007), *By These Hands: Portraits from the Factory Floor* (2002), and *Stolen Dreams: Portraits of Working Children* (1997).

David Parker's photography presentation and talk was an epiphany for Beth. She said: "The impact of seeing those pictures put me over the hump of being involved. It was eye opening. The sheer issues were a motivating factor. What it comes down to is my background."

Beth feels that her family upbringing lay the groundwork for future activism. They did a lot together as a family. Small things like dinner every night where they shared conversations about their days. They went to church on Sunday as a family and did pizza and movies on Saturdays. Beth said:

> The Catholic faith has a real emphasis on social justice and service to others. As a family, we did can and bottle drives, coat drives, simple service projects. We were planning to go to Disney World as a family and we had saved up the money. Then my Mom received a video in the mail from Catholic Relief Services. It was about people in the Dominican Republic not having shelter. My Mom played it for us and we decided to donate the money instead of going to Disney. We built three houses in the Dominican Republic.

William feels that the 7th-grade curriculum during Beth's era also played an important role. They studied the Industrial Revolution and illustrated its impact though a study of the Lowell millworkers. They did a play about the millworkers and Ron took the students to Boote Cotton Mills Museum in Lowell and taught them about child labor. Beth gave her first speech at a teacher's workshop at the Lowell Museum on December 4, 1997. Beth and her classmates shared Iqbal's story and spoke about the problems faced by child laborers around the world.

At her first speech Beth felt that Mr. Adams could tell that she was comfortable speaking in public. However, he never appointed her to the role. Whenever a speaking engagement came in he would have interested students write something on the topic. They would give mini speeches and the students would vote to select the students who would represent them.

Beth's sense of agency and competence were enhanced by her role as spokesperson. When her peers selected her to speak, Beth said it made her feel "ecstatic" and did wonders for her self-confidence. In addition, her parents were totally supportive. They would rearrange their schedules so they could drive and/or chaperone the group when they went on speaking engagements.

Before Beth entered high school, she had spoken at major venues. On May 3, 1997, she served on the Youth Power Panel at the National Consumer League's Child Labor Coalition Biennial Conference in Orlando, Florida. She delivered a speech at the Harvard Graduate School of Education the following September. In October, she traveled to Washington, DC to accept the National Consumer League's Trumpeter Award on behalf of The Kid's Campaign to Build a School for Iqbal.

In 1994, Reggie Lewis, former Celtics Captain, and Jon Jennings, Assistant Celtics Coach, joined forces with the Anti-Defamation League and Blue Cross Blue Shield to create Team Harmony, a series of events that would bring middle and high school students together to fight bigotry and hatred. The Kid's Campaign to Build a School for Iqbal was given the Team Harmony Global Activism Award in December 1998. Beth was elected to accept the award and give a speech to over 11,000 middle and high school students and their teachers.

Beth's younger sister Mary was in 6th grade and a new member of ODW. She said, "We all went on stage. I think that we were the only group that did that. Beth spoke and we sort of surrounded her ... which was cool. Beth was up on the big screen."

Beth ended the year with a trip to DC where she addressed a Congressional Roundtable on Youth Activism. She said:

> Mr. Adams is amazing in such a subtle way. He gave me so much confidence and made me feel like I was a great speaker and then of course the class selected me. I gained so much confidence from my experiences with ODW and the Kid's Campaign. It helped me with my interpersonal skills. We were meeting all the time. I interacted with media and with adults. My public speaking skills improved.
>
> My parents had always emphasized how important education was but ODW and the Kid's Campaign put it in a more real light. I was inspired to work really, really hard in school, continue on with my education and not take it for granted. I started to see education more as a privilege than a right.
>
> I thought the more academic success I could get the more opportunities I would have to make a difference. I associated my involvement in ODW and the Kid's Campaign with how much success I could achieve. Without this I wouldn't have had a sense of what kind of difference I could make. I felt limitless at his point.

Beth: High School Activism

Beth attended Archbishop Williams (Archie's), a Catholic High School in Braintree. She still had younger siblings at Broad Meadows and continued to represent the Kid's Campaign and ODW as a spokesperson against child labor. In February of her freshman year, Beth spoke at a Peace and Justice seminar at Wellesley College. At the end of the year, she decided to try and start an ODW chapter at her high school.

Beth approached a 9th-grade history teacher, Meryl Baxter, and spoke with her about starting an ODW group. Baxter, who is now a Dean at the School, signed on as the group advisor and Beth was able to recruit nine other students to start the program.

The group at Archie's followed a similar format to that at ODW Broad Meadows; however, they did not meet on a weekly basis or engage in as many activities. In the fall, they received the proposals and met twice: once to read the proposal and discuss the proposals' merits and a second time to vote. They submitted their vote electronically to the national ODW Director. They met several other times to educate themselves about the country and the project. The workday was a school beautification project. Every year in the spring, the students would volunteer a Saturday to work to improve the school grounds. They used a pledge system and collected funds for the ODW project, based upon the number of hours that they worked.

At the end of the school year Beth was invited to serve on a panel on "Providing and Improving Basic Education and Access" at the National Consumer League's Child Labor Biennial Conference. She traveled to Washington, DC with Mr. Adams to present.

Beth's most memorable speaking engagement, however, came during her junior year when she was invited to speak at the United Nations in March 2001. She presented a 30-minute speech followed by a 15-minute question and answer session to 900 youth delegates from all over the world at the 25th anniversary of the UN International School Conference. Beth's emerging global consciousness is evident in the transcript of her speech.

Poverty is the main cause of child exploitation. However, ending poverty or ending child labor is not just as simple as building schools or raising money. No, we have to educate people that ending child labor is very complex. In fact we believe that the solution to ending child labor is at least five layers deep:

1. Education: ALL children must go to school until at least their 14th birthday.
2. Governments: Governments must pass AND enforce laws to protect children.
3. Corporations: (like Nike, Disney and others) must take full responsibility for guaranteeing that no children are working in the factories or in the fields.
4. Consumers: (like you and me) labels must tell if something is child labor free. How else can we shop?
5. Poverty: small microcredit loans must be made available to poor families so they can start their own small businesses.

Everyday millions of children are forced to go to work. Did you ever stop to think that a malnourished, beaten child could have made the shirt that you are wearing?

Beth felt that the UN speech gave the fledging ODW program at Archie's credibility with the students and faculty and helped it to gain momentum. However, active membership never grew beyond 15 in a given year. Beth believes that the problem is due in part to the large number of competing activities and time commitment required by high school sports. She also feels that it is difficult to find an adult mentor as willing to devote the time and energy as Mr. Adams.

Beth: College Activism

Beth attended the College of Worchester in Worchester, Massachusetts. She loved reading and writing and knew that she wanted to be an English teacher. She majored in English and enrolled in their teacher education certification program. She said:

> I wanted to follow in Mr. Adams footsteps ... helping others and English. I thought that I could make as much of an impact as he did. In my head that was the course that I wanted to take. Now, as a teacher, I realize how difficult it is.

Beth knew that the College of Worchester required that the students do their student teaching in an urban public school. This was part of the reason she chose the program. Working in an urban school appealed to her sense of social justice and she feels that she gained a great deal from the experience.

At the College, Beth enrolled in the Spring break service immersion program. Each year students in this program traveled to a different location to do service work. She went to West Virginia, Kentucky, twice and to New Orleans after Hurricane Katrina. Service varied from physical labor to reading to children. For example, in New Orleans, they cleaned out houses that had been ruined by the flood. They did painting and built ramps to make the building wheelchair accessible.

Because of The Kid's Campaign and ODW, Beth always wanted to travel abroad. She wanted to witness the poverty and injustice that she had been fighting against firsthand. She had this opportunity during her sophomore year. She traveled to Papua New Guinea with Habitat for Humanity International during her January break and spent three and a half weeks building houses. She lived in a village that had no electricity or running water. She spent a lot of time observing, listening, and getting to know the villagers and the challenges they faced.

Upon graduation, Beth took a job as 8th-grade middle school teacher in Kingston, Massachusetts, at the Silver Lake Regional Middle School. In the 2007–2008 school year she started an ODW program at the school.

Mary

Mary is 2 years younger than Beth. She learned about ODW from her big sister and decided to follow her lead. She said, "My older sister, Beth was already at Broad Meadows. I just followed suit. She came home and talked about it. I had participated in a work day at a younger age; tagging along."

Like Beth, Mary feels that she was drawn to ODW because it reinforced the values that were emphasized at home. She said:

> Our Catholic background played a big role in the way that we were brought up. We were always taught to be kind, generous, giving, to volunteer our time and to use our gift and talents for the well-being of everyone. We were brought up with a close family connection.

Mary was shyer than Beth. She was not as comfortable speaking in public. Mr. Adams helped Mary and other novice ODW students transition to the role of public speaker by first doing short segments of a speech and then gradually moving to longer speaking segments. Mary felt that she gained confidence because she had an ally and role model in her older sister. They would practice speaking and writing speeches at home.

Mary's first speaking engagement was at Harvard Graduate School of Education in September 1998 when she was in 6th grade. Her sister Beth was the main speaker. Mary told the story of a young boy in a developing country who made Kool-Aid and became ill from the pesticides in the water supply. This gradual entrance into the arena of public speaking enhanced her sense of agency and competence.

In 8th grade Mary spoke at the United Nations Rose Gala at a conference spearheading the Year of the Volunteer with her sister Laura, 2 years her junior. Mary sees this event as the pinnacle of her activism. She said:

> That was quite the event. They had a cocktail hour, with appetizers an ice sculpture. My Dad was with us and Mr. Adams. Glen Close was the MC and Kofi Annan also spoke. Then we spoke about building the school in Pakistan and our efforts through ODW to expand an orphanage in El Salvador.
>
> It was the most nervous that I ever was. Reporters took our pictures while we were speaking and we had to be prepared to speak to anyone. For me it is a lot easier to write something down and memorize it than it is to talk on the spot. We practiced panel questions and interviews. We learned how to respond on our feet. That taught us about professionalism.

Mary attended Providence College where she majored in Elementary and Special Education. She currently teaches 3rd grade at Snug Harbor Elementary School in the Germantown section of Quincy. Her participation in ODW helped to inspire Mary to choose to teach in a school in the projects.

She feels that her participation in ODW and Mr. Adams' mentoring has influenced her career. She acquired leadership skills and is more apt to be the person in the group who is willing to get up and present. This served her well in high school when she was doing projects and in college, especially in practicum and student teaching. Mary feels that she learned professionalism, confidence, vocabulary, and public speaking as a whole. However, the organizational skills that she learned have most influenced her own teaching. She said:

> Being able to prepare and present things in an organized way … prioritize things … informs the way that I teach because I was able to learn so much through the way Mr. Adams taught. I try to model through my actions and do a lot of group work.
>
> I let students bounce ideas off of each other, without stepping in and telling them what to do. I let them figure things out for themselves and almost sneakily guide them.
>
> Participation in ODW has shaped the person I am professionally and overall. Every aspect of what I do is rooted in my upbringing initially and the experiences I was able to have because of Mr. Adams and Broad Meadows. That led me to the choices that I made and the choices that I make every day as an educator.

Kristen and Tom

Beth, Mary, and Laura's younger siblings Kristen and Tom were also active participants in the ODW community. Both started in the group when they were in the 5th grade. Kristen who is two years older than Tom said:

> I was a fifth grader and my older sisters were involved. I was hearing about the projects that they were working on and that is what sparked my interest. So I asked Mr. Adams if I could start going to the meetings. During 5th grade, I was just taking it in and listening and once I entered middle school I started taking a more active role.

Like their older siblings, Kristen and Tom felt that their participation was linked to the values emphasized in their family that were rooted in Catholicism. They believed that their parents supported and encouraged their participation. Tom said:

> If you are doing something like speaking and you see your parent there, it makes you feel encouraged; especially being so young. My parents would do a lot of behind the scenes stuff too. Like any function ODW would have either my Mom or Dad would be there supporting us.

Kristen had many inspiring experiences as a participant in the ODW community. She attended the Reebok Human Rights Awards and spoke at the opening of the Reebok's Child Care Center in New York when she was in the 6th grade. She met with Cedza Dimani, Nelson Mandela's grandson, when she was in 8th grade. Dimani, a student at Tufts, came to Quincy to meet with ODW representatives to congratulate them on their work and speak with them about the UN Millennium Development Goals.

The summer before Kristen entered 9th grade she presented at the Workshop on Child Labor for Educators with her brother Tom. For Tom presenting at the workshop was a pivotal experience. He said:

> That was the summer, I was going into 7th grade. I was speaking about the program with Kristen and we were in a room full of distinguished adults and it just felt powerful that we captivated the room. The President of the National Education Association was there and so was Kailash Satyarthi. When I listened to Kailash's stories about his work rescuing child laborers, it was so moving.

Kristen interjected, "It's those inspiring moments that make you feel like you are a part of something larger."

Both Kristen and Tom felt that one of the best things about ODW was that it was student led. They said that it provided them with a learning experience that was totally different from anything they had experienced previously. Kristen explained:

> I liked the student run aspect of it because it was really empowering It broke from the traditional forms of education that we were accustomed to. I learned so much through participating in ODW. It was a different way of learning, a much more active approach It was so different and so eye-opening that you could accomplish so much by yourself.
>
> Mr. Adams would always say "Its student run." and we would always have to figure things out which is not typical. Even if we ran into a road block or something didn't go our way, we would have to figure things out and then proceed based on what we decided to do. I think that was my favorite part, having that power and being able to make decisions.

Tom liked the diversity of the ODW community and felt that it "transcended the social hierarchy" of middle school. Anyone could join and have a role, so students who weren't athletes or part of the popular crowd could find a safe space to participate. Kristen said that when students initially came up to middle school they tend to sit with the kids with whom they went to the neighborhood elementary school. ODW provided her with one of the first opportunities to meet and interact with students from different parts of town.

By participating in ODW, both Kristen and Tom felt that they developed public speaking, communication, and organizational skills. Kristen said:

Communication skills, coordinating projects and getting things done were big. If we were having an affair to raise money, we'd have to contact companies and local businesses to donate things and I learned how to communicate with people other than my peers.

Tom believes that in addition to the skills he developed he gained perspective. He said:

The one main thing that I learned was not to take anything for granted. When I would think about the kids that we were trying to help, it would be a reminder that I had it made compared to other people.

Both Kristen and Tom attended Archbishop Williams High School and participated in the ODW chapter at the school that their sister Beth had started there. Kristen went on a service trip to Haiti through her church during her junior year. They attended Providence College where they were both studying to be teachers. At the time of the interview Tom was a sophomore studying to be a history teacher and Kristen was a senior studying elementary education.

Tom said that his family was the main influence for his career choice. He said:

My friends tell me I am not going to make any money as a teacher. I just look at it right now, at this point in my life, both my parents were around. I can't remember a time in high school that my Dad missed a sporting event and there are seven of us. We had a comfortable life.

However, Mr. Adams and his experience in ODW have strongly influenced how he would like to teach. He was most impressed by Mr. Adams' interdisciplinary approach and the fact that he never taught to the test. He said:

Seventh grade is the year you have to take the MCATS. That is the big test for Massachusetts and you have to pass it. We would never do practice tests or anything like that. We wouldn't even mention the MCATS. We would just do different things, not necessarily unconventional things. He would never teach to the test and the results were staggering. It's a tribute to him as an educator.

Kristen felt that her family, ODW, and Mr. Adams all had an impact on her career choice. She said, "I always wanted to have a career where I could make a difference. You know Mr. Adams impacted our lives so much and I want to be able to have an impact on others."

Kristen and Tom view citizenship in terms of service and feel that good citizens are individuals who see themselves as a part of a whole and are willing to contribute. They feel that their identity as global, national, and/or local citizen is context specific and depends upon the circumstances at hand. They try to be conscious consumers. Neither will buy Nike products and they try to buy fair trade whenever possible. Kristen said: "ODW is something that is just part of you. It opened doors. You are always a member."

Kristen is now a 4th-grade teacher at Parker Elementary School in Quincy. Tom teaches 7th-grade Social Studies at Broad Meadows. The ODW chapter that Beth started at Silver Lake Middle School is entering its 8th year.

CONCLUSION

ODW played an important role in the lives of Mike, Rita, Mai, Beth, Mary, Kristen, and Tom. As in the cases of Amanda, Jen, and Ellaine, participation in The Kid's Campaign or ODW enhanced their senses of agency, civic efficacy, and competence and helped to shape their identities. While all of the students came from homes where doing well in school was stressed, the importance placed upon activism and/or service varied significantly. Amanda, Jen, Ellaine, Rita, and Mia developed their activism and sense of civic efficacy from participation in The Kid's Campaign or ODW. Activism and civic service were not emphasized at home.

Beth, Mary, Tom, and Kristen were drawn to the Campaign and ODW because it mirrored and reinforced ideals and behaviors that were modeled in the home. Mike came from a home where service and civic efficacy were modeled by his mother through her work. This difference, I believe, could account for variation in the participants' accounts of the impact of the programs on their lives.

Like their predecessors in The Kid's Campaign, participation in the ODW community provided Rita and Mia with exposure to a variety of adult roles and the opportunity to try out these roles and develop the associated skills. The experience influenced their choices of career and college majors. In addition, like Amanda, Jen, and Ellaine, Rita and Mia were able to develop their communications, managerial and public relations skills at the university but were not able to find employment that would allow them to use these skills for social change. They currently work in the private sector.

For Mike and the members of the B family career choice and major were linked strongly to their home experiences. Participation in ODW reinforced these values and provided them opportunities to develop the types of 21st-century skills that would help them to succeed. In Mike's case, Mr. Adams and ODW provided him with the confidence in his academic abilities at a critical point in his education. For Beth, Mary, Kristen, and Tom, ODW provided a venue and a way of imagining how the ideals and values that had been instilled at home could be put into practice. Mr. Adams served as the role model, the teacher they would emulate to achieve these ends in their own careers.

While the sample size is small, these cases do not conform to research findings on civic engagement. Much of the research indicates civic engagement and youth activism are linked to socioeconomic status. Students from upper middle class backgrounds are the most likely to become involved and are provided with opportunities for meaningful participation (Flanagan & Levine 2010). McIntosh, Hart, and Youniss (2007) found that activism and engagement are linked to frequent discussion of political issues at home.

Political discussion was not a part of the participants' family lives. In addition the interviewees' conceptions of a good citizen did not include typical responses, such as voting, obeying the law, following political issues, working on political campaigns (Torney-Purta & The International Association for the Evaluation of Educational Achievement, 2001). Respondents' definitions seem to be influenced by participation in The Kid's Campaign and/or ODW as they saw good citizens as individuals who worked for the greater good at the local, national, or global level.

All of the interviewees believe that their experiences in these after school communities enhanced their understanding and awareness of the world. As consumers they honor Iqbal's memory and Mr. Adams' teachings as adults as they continue to check labels and buy fair trade whenever possible. These are practices that they will share with their children and their future students.

Conclusion

Every student campaign seems unique but the constant is connecting kids to the larger world. It is an attempt to provide students with real-world experiences, meaningful to the student, and the opportunity to apply skills learned in class. Ironically, application, a true understanding of learning, is not measured by the high-stakes state testing nor by teacher evaluations. Still, it is the right thing to do.

As teachers, in our planning and in our teaching, we need to be disciplined enough to always save room for the student voice.

RON ADAMS

The Kid's Campaign and ODW have provided middle school students with authentic educational experiences of a global nature for over twenty years. These experiences move beyond the realm of practice fields. They are not teacher-created activities, problems, or projects that simulate practice for some future time, but actual real-life problems that the students must solve.

As stated previously, Tony Wagner (2008) has argued quite passionately that American students need to develop what he refers to as "survival skills" to both compete in the increasingly globalized economy and solve problems of a global nature that we face and will continue to face as the 21st century progresses. I can think of no better way to develop skills such as critical thinking and problem solving, collaboration, initiative, effective oral and written communication, accessing and analyzing information than to provide students with opportunities to solve real-life problems that require students to develop these skills in communities of practice.

In the current educational climate where learning is becoming increasingly decontextualized and linked to standardized tests, it is imperative to provide students with opportunities to engage with real-world problems in school or in after school settings. The experiences of Ron and his students in The Kid's Campaign and ODW provide insight as to how to construct enduring real-life programs that are global in nature and have impact at both the global and the local level. The structural designs that evolved in these successful programs can be used in other contexts.

Both programs created communities of practice that provided real opportunities for youth to participate, voice their concerns, and share in the decision-making process. While decision making was democratic and the organization was run by students, the relationship between the students and the teacher mentor resembled the youth-centered apprenticeship identified by Kirshner (2006). Ron took on the role of facilitator. However, when the students lacked the expertise needed to pursue a goal, such as speech writing, he would jump in and provide enough guidance by modeling and coaching the needed skills and then fade into the background and resume his facilitator role. He also helped students make contacts in the adult world and provided background information when needed.

In ODW, these background information sessions and events such as accompanying veterans on speaking engagements and participating in the organization of fund-raisers provided meaningful experiences for newcomers interested in becoming more involved in the organization and allowed veterans to take on mentorship roles, thereby enhancing expertise and identification. Creating significant experiences for newcomers that provide pathways to full membership (legitimate peripheral participation) is critical for attracting new members and maintaining a vital, functioning community that continues as students graduate and the one-time newcomers take the helm.

Equally important is creating a shared feeling of purpose, a sense of community history, and a shared repertoire of cultural resources that maintain the community. The repetition of common stories creates a sense of shared history. At Broad Meadows two stories—the history of activism at Broad Meadows and the Iqbal story—are retold over the course of the year and are a source of pride to the participants. In addition, the community has developed insider gestures (the ODW greeting), symbols (Ducky, the ODW T-shirt), ways of doing things (analyzing NGO proposals), rituals and routines (the hot cocoa sale, Penny Power day's work, T-shirt ceremony).

Stories, symbols, and events are essential for shaping identity and help to make educational experiences truly transformative.

Learning about the ramifications of global inequality can be daunting at any age. The shared stories and activities provide the students with role models and examples of tangible actions that people like themselves have used effectively to create change in the past. One of the most interesting innovations of ODW Broad Meadows is the education the students receive through ongoing collaboration with partner nonprofit NGOs. Organizations like Goodweave provide the students with an inside view of child labor in the rug weaving industry and attempt at solutions that are currently underway. They meet activists like Nina Smith who have dedicated their lives to ending child labor, and interact with child laborers via Skype who are young adolescents like themselves. These types of experiences help the middle school students see the value of their work and feel part of something larger than themselves.

Providing students with opportunities to solve real-life problems exposes them to career opportunities that they might not have known about or considered. It allows them to try out roles like publicist, business manager, speech writer, public relations expert and helps them imagine a broader range of future options.

Ron Adams retired in June 2016. He worked as a teacher for 41 consecutive years; 33 of them at Broad Meadows Middle School. In collaboration with his students, he developed innovative programs that benefited his students and helped their peers in developing nations around the world. These programs and program structures can be used and adapted by other educators to allow students to participate in meaningful real-world experiences in the classroom or after school programs.

Ron's career is a testimony to what teachers can accomplish when they are encouraged and supported, allowed to " team and dream," and form classroom and/or afterschool communities that are responsive to student concerns and allow them to investigate global issues that touch them deeply. If Americans want schools that foster initiative, creativity, collaboration, problem solving, and global competence, then we must foster and support the same skills in our teachers. Only by empowering our teachers and allowing them the freedom to create can they in turn empower our students.

Appendix

ODW Annual Projects

2015–2016
Country: Haiti
NGO: Alliance for Children Foundation; http://www.afcfoundation.org
Project Description: Provide support for 80 children living in an orphanage in Kenscoff, Haiti. This includes sustaining the feeding program, providing tuition so that school-age children can attend school, and maintaining orphanage learning center. Providing training for teachers who work at the facility in preschool and after school programs.

2014–2015
Country: Zimbabwe
NGO: American Foundation for Children Affected by AIDS; http://www.afcaids.org
Project Description: Contribute to the livelihood security for 36 families comprised of orphaned and/or vulnerable children affected by AIDS. The families will be provided with livestock, seeds, and training in animal medical care, nutrition, and gardening.

2013–2014
Country: India
NGO: Good Weave; www.GoodWeave.org
Project Description: Provide resources for 250 poor children, mostly girls, to attend a nonformal school in Uttar Pradesh province. The school has been named the "ODW School."

2012–2013
Country: Kenya

NGO: The Kenyan School House Project; http://www.kenyanschoolhouse.org
Project Description: Provide tuition, books, meals, health care for 18 months
for the 38 students enrolled in The Kenyan School House Project.

2011–2012
Country: Nepal
NGO: Good Weave; www.GoodWeave.org
Project Description: Provide education, room and board, counseling, and
health care for 40 rescued child laborers.

2010–2011
Country: Ethiopia
NGO: Selamta Family Project; www.selamtafamilyproject.org/
Project Description: Build four group homes for children who were orphaned
by AIDS, and living in an orphanage. Hired foster moms and aunts to staff
group homes.

2009–2010
Country: Haiti
NGO: Partners in Health; www.pih.org
Project Description: Provide vaccinations and scholarships for 100 children
living in poverty in rural Haiti.

2008–2009
Country: Burundi
NGO: Village Health Works, www.villagehealthworks.org
Project Description: Help complete and staff a brand new health clinic for
victims of genocide in Burundi and Rwanda.

2007–2008
Country: Ethiopia
NGO: Selamta Family Project; www.selamtafamilyproject.org/
Project Description: Construct 7 new group homes for children who were
orphaned by AIDS: Hired 7 foster moms and 7 foster aunts to staff homes
and create family environment for children who were living in orphanages.

2006–2007
Country: Rwanda
NGO: CHABHA, Project Independence; www.CHABHA.org.
Project Description: Provide vocational training and scholarships for 88 high
school students living in poverty, so that they can obtain jobs such as chefs,
carpenters, and electricians.

2005–2006
Country: Vietnam
NGO: Heifer International; www.heifer.org
Project Description: Provide vocational training to 40 parents of young girls at risk for becoming child laborers and well as education for the girls themselves.

2004–2005 (Multiple mini projects)
Countries: Rwanda, Kenya, Israel an Vietnam
$2,000 for Rwandan orphans; $3,000 for Kenyan Health Clinic; $600 for Israeli youth; $2000 for Vietnamese girls
NGOs: numerous
Projects: numerous

2003–2004
Country: Bangladesh
NGO: Volunteers Association for Bangladesh; www.vabonline.org/
Project Description: Provide scholarships for 80 high school students living in poverty as well as renovate their school building.

2002–2003
Country: Ethiopia
NGO: A Glimmer of Hope Foundation; www.aglimmerofhope.org
Project Description: Renovate a closed middle and elementary school.

2001–2002 (2 projects) ODW USA raised $40,000 for a school project in Nepal
Country: Nepal
NGO: Educate the Children-Nepal; etc-nepal.org
Project Descriptions: Provide scholarships for girls living in poverty to attend school. (The literacy rate for girls is below 30%.)
Country: USA
NGO: Twin Towers Orphan's Fund; www.ttof.org/
Project Description: Provide for trauma counseling and scholarships for US children orphaned by the 9–11 attacks on America.

2000–2001
Country: El Salvador
NGO: Salesian Missions: www.salesianmissions.org/
Project Description: Doubled the size of Ciudad De Los Niño's, an orphanage that was experiencing severe overcrowding as a result of the Civil War.

1999–2001
Country: Haiti
NGO: CARE and World Concern Development; www.CARE.org
Project Description: Provide livestock and literacy training for poor, rural Haitian children.

References

Adams, R. (2007, November 21). Iqbal Forum–What do store managers know about child labor? Retrieved from http://mirrorimage.com/yabb/YaBB.pl?num= 1195684307/2

Andrews, P. G., & Conk, J. A. (2012). The World Awaits: Building Global Competence in the Middle Grades. *Middle School Journal, 44*(1), 54–63. doi:10.1080/00 940771.2012.11461840

Atwell, N. (1987). *In the middle: Writing, reading, and learning with adolescents.* Upper Montclair, NJ: Boynton/Cook.

Barab, S., & Duffy, T. (2012). From practice fields to communities of practice. In *Theoretical foundations of learning environments* (pp. 20–65). New York, NY: Routledge.

Barber, T. (2007). Young people and civic participation: A conceptual review. *Youth an Policy, 96,* 19–36.

Brustad, M. R. (2014). *Solidarity projects in Norwegian schools: Students motivation and school leaders' rationale* (Master's thesis, University of Oslo, Oslo, Norway). Retrieved from /www.duo.uio.no/bitstream/handle/10852/41291/Mphil-thesis-CIE--Maja-R--Brustad.pdf?sequence=1

Daniels, H. (1994). *Literature circles: Voice and choice in the student-centered classroom.* York, ME: Stenhouse Publishers.

Flanagan, C., & Levine, P. (2010). Civic engagement and the transition to adulthood. *The Future of Children, 20*(1), 159–179. doi:10.1353/foc.0.0043

George, P., & Alexander, W. (2003). *The exemplary middle school.* Belmont, CA: Thomson/Wadsworth.

Global labor practice: Company information Eddie Bauer. (2015). Retrieved June 25, 2015, from http://www.eddiebauer.com/company-info/company-info-global-labor-practice.jsp

Goodweave: About the organization. (2016). Retrieved from http://www.goodweave. org/index.php?cid=107

International Labor Organization (ILO). (2002). *A future without child labor: Global report under the follow-up to the ILO declaration on fundamental principles and rights at work. Report of the Director-General, 2002.* ILO.

Jackson, A., Davis, G., Abeel, M., & Bordonaro, A. (2000). *Turning points 2000: educating adolescents in the 21st century.* New York, NY: Teachers College Press.

Junior Scholastic. (2006, October 16). *The world in focus: Fast facts on 194 countries.* Retrieved from http://www.the free library.com/_/print/PrintArticle. aspx?id=153706680

Kirshner, B. (2006). Apprenticeship Learning in Youth Activism. In S. Ginwright, P. Noguera, & J. Cammarota (Eds.), *Beyond resistance: Youth activism and community change: New democratic possibilities for practice* (pp. 37–58). New York, NY: Routledge.

Kohn, A. (1993). Choices for Children: Why and How to Let Students Decide. *Phi Delta Kappan, 75*(1).

Kuklin, S. (1998). *Iqbal Masih and the crusaders against child slavery.* New York: H. Holt and Co.

Larson, R., Walker, K., & Pearce, N. (2005). A Comparison of Youth-driven and Adult-driven Youth Programs: Balancing Inputs from Youth and Adults. *Journal of Community Psychology, 33*(1), 57–74. doi:10.1002/jcop.20035

Lave, J., & Wenger, E. (1991). *Situated learning: Legitimate peripheral participation.* Cambridge [England]: Cambridge University Press.

LeCompte, M. D., & Schensul, J. J. (1999). *Analyzing & interpreting ethnographic data.* Walnut Creek, CA: AltaMira Press.

Mansilla, V. B., & Jackson, A. (2011). *Educating for global competence: Preparing our youth to engage the world.* Retrieved from http://asiasociety.org/files/book-globalcompetence.pdf

McIntosh, H., Hart, D., & Youniss, J. (2007). The Influence of Family Political Discussion on Youth Civic Development: Which Parent Qualities Matter? *PS: Political Science & Politics, 40*(03), 495–499.

Mitra, D. L., & Serriere, S. C. (2012). Student Voice in Elementary School Reform: Examining Youth Development in Fifth Graders. *American Educational Research Journal, 49*(4), 743-774. doi:10.3102/0002831212443079

National Peace Corps Association. (2003, January/February). NetAid world class game aims at education for every child. *Global teachnet,* 11. Retrieved from http://www.peacecorpsconnect.org/wordpress/wp-content/uploads/2010/07/GTN-JanFeb03.pdf

Nehring, J. (2009). *The practice of school reform: Lessons from two centuries.* Albany, NY: SUNY Press.

O'Donoghue, J. L., Krishner, B., McLaughin. (2002). Introduction: Moving Youth Participation Forward. *New Directions for Youth Development, 96,* 15–26.

ODW Broad Meadows. (2004, July 29). Child-Labor-Free-Shopping Trip. Retrieved from http://mirrorimage.com/updates/01–05update.html

Operasjon Dagsverk, Ostfold. (n.d.). Ditt distrikt > Østfold - Operasjon Dagsverk. Retrieved January 28, 2015, from http://www.od.no/Ditt_distrikt/_stfold

Operasjon Dagsverk. (2008, August 28). What is Operation Dayswork?–Operasjon Dagsverk. Retrieved from http://www.od.no/noop/page.php?p=Artikler/964. html&d=1

Operasjon Dagsverk. (n.d.). NPD history. Retrieved January 27, 2015, from http://www.od.no/

Operasjon Dagsverk. (n.d.). Om OD > OD-systemet–Operasjon Dagsverk. Retrieved January 27, 2015, from http://www.od.no/Om_OD/OD_systemet/index.html

Operation Day's Work, USA. (1999, July). Quest CC03: ODW Mission Statement and the ODW Constitutional Development. Retrieved from http://www.solarquest.com/schoolhouse/quest.asp?id=1751

Operation Day's Work, USA. (2014). Blank Grant Application « Operation Days Work/ The Quincy Kids. Retrieved from http://www.odw-usa.org/blank-grant-application/

Parker, W. (2003). *Teaching Democracy Unity and Diversity in Public Life*. New York, NY: Teacher's College Press.

Quest CC02: Christon Domond: Reflecting on Haiti. (1999, July 10). Retrieved from http://www.solarquest.com/school/quest.asp?id=1746

Quincy Historical Society. (2007). *Four centuries of new Americans: Residents, immigrants, and heritage in Quincy*. Retrieved from http://file:///C:/Users/Owner/Downloads/immigbrochreadlayout.pdf

Seidman, I. (2006). *Interviewing as qualitative research: A guide for researchers in education and the social sciences* (3rd ed.). New York, NY: Teachers College Press.

Semaan, G., & Yamazaki, K. (2015). The Relationship Between Global Competence and Language Learning Motivation: An Empirical Study in Critical Language Classrooms. *Foreign Language Annals*, *48*(3), 511–520. doi:10.1111/flan.12146

Shier, H. (2001). Pathways to participation: openings, opportunities and obligations. *Children & Society*, *15*, 107–117. doi:10.1002/chi.617

Shier, H. (2006). Pathways to Participation Revisited: Nicaragua Perspective. *New Zealand Association for Intermediate and Middle Schooling*, (2), 14–19.

Silvers, J. (1996, February). Child labor in Pakistan. *Atlantic Monthly*, *17*(2).

Torney-Purta, J., & International Association for the Evaluation of Educational Achievement. (2001). *Citizenship and education in twenty-eight countries: Civic knowledge and engagement at age fourteen*. Amsterdam: International Association for the Evaluation of Educational Achievement.

Trilling, B., Fadel, C., & Partnership for 21st Century Skills. (2009). *21st century skills: Learning for life in our times*. San Francisco, CA: Jossey-Bass.

Video of Iqbal's visit to Broad Meadows Middle School[VHS]. (1994).

Wagner, T. (2008). *The global achievement gap: Why even our best schools don't teach the new survival skills our children need-- and what we can do about it*. New York, NY: Basic Books.

Wenger, E. (1998). *Communities of Practice: Learning, Meaning, and Identity*. Cambridge, UK: Cambridge University Press.

Zeisler, J. (1999, July). *Operation Day's Work constitutional convention*. Retrieved from www.solarquest.com/schoolhouse/school.asp?id=317

About the Author

Linda Kantor Swerdlow is an associate professor of education in the Master of Arts in Teaching Program at Drew University. Her specialization is history, social studies, and global education. She has written articles in her field, presented at national and international conferences, and organized a regional conference on Teaching about Global Child Labor and Human Trafficking.